EARLY VISITORS TO HAWORTH

From Ellen Nussey to Virginia Woolf

HAWORTH, YORKSHIRE

The village of Haworth, the scene of the labours of the Rev. William Grimshaw, a contemporary and friend of the Rev. John Wesley, is situated on a somewhat lofty eminence near the desolate moors which divide the counties of York and Lancaster. It has been supposed that the first syllable of the name is a corruption of 'high,' and that the second means 'a farm or cultivated spot,' – a derivation perfectly agreeable with the position of the village, as well as with its general character; for 'there are few places in England', says one, 'which present such a striking example of the mastery of man over the most intractable, barren, and inhospitable spots.'

The Christian Miscellany,
Vol. IV – *Second Series* – January, 1858.

EARLY VISITORS TO HAWORTH

From Ellen Nussey to Virginia Woolf

Selected and edited by Charles Lemon

Foreword by Lord Briggs of Lewes

With best wishes
Charles Lemon

The Brontë Society

Published by The Brontë Society, Brontë Parsonage Museum,
Haworth, Keighley, West Yorkshire BD22 8DR

Typeset and printed in Great Britain by Alden,
Oxford, Didcot and Northampton

ISBN 0-9505829-6-4

CONTENTS

ILLUSTRATIONS

ABBREVIATIONS

BPM	Brontë Parsonage Museum
BST	Brontë Society *Transactions*
SHB	*The Brontës: Their Lives, Friendships and Correspondence* ed. by T. J. Wise and J. A. Symington, 4 vols. Shakespeare Head Brontë, Oxford, 1932.

ACKNOWLEDGMENTS

For help in compiling this anthology I must single out the following with my grateful thanks: Dr Robert Barnard, Ian Dewhirst, Ann Dinsdale, Bob Duckett, Sarah Fermi, Margaret Smith, Kathryn White, Barbara Whitehead and Keighley Reference Library (who provided the maps).

I am also grateful for permission granted by Mr J. Copley, Dr Timothy Foley, Mr H.C. Harden, Mrs Phoebe Rankin, Professor Kathleen Tillotson, Random House UK Ltd. and Smith College, Northampton, Massachusetts, to include in these pages contributions previously published in Brontë Society *Transactions*.

Certain of the illustrations are reproduced by kind permission of the following – the National Portrait Gallery, London, pp. 20, 23 and 51; the Public Record Office, London, pp. 33 and 104; Simon Warner, Stanbury, p. 71; and the Knowle Funeral Service, Keighley, p. 87. The remainder are from the Brontë Society Collection.

Finally I am greatly indebted to John Martins, my son-in-law, for his ready help in solving my word processing problems.

Charles Lemon

FOREWORD

Charles Lemon's impressive and detailed knowledge of the Brontës extends, as any such knowledge must, to an equally impressive and detailed knowledge of the environment in which they lived and moved. The Brontë Society, whose centenary history he wrote, owes an immense debt to him both for his research and for his commitment, and I am proud as President to write this brief foreword to his book.

What the Victorians thought and felt about travel was central to their own conceptions of communication and culture. Time and distance were cut, speed was accelerated. A new map of Europe, even of the world, was charted. Literary associations enhanced a new sense of place. Very soon after the writings of the Brontës became known Haworth found its place on that map, attracting visitors from near and far away. For some visitors crossing the Atlantic was the prelude. For some twentieth-century visitors, living through new phases of a continuing communications revolution, crossing the Pacific Ocean is the starting point.

In this book Charles Lemon draws on a great range and variety of sources, going back to the beginnings. Impressions vary too. People were changing as well as places. Virginia Woolf saw people and places through very different eyes from Elizabeth Gaskell. The power to communicate place was strong, of course, in both cases. Most of the thousands of people who visit the Parsonage and the village in the late-twentieth century are content with a postcard. Yet I am sure that Haworth figures in innumerable journals and diaries as it does in a surprisingly large number of novels and poems.

The same place can mean very different things to different people which was one of the themes of my book *Victorian Cities* in which Bradford figures. For me Haworth is part of a scene to which I belonged as a child. Boys from Haworth were at Keighley Grammar School during the 1930s and I knew many of them. The moors for me were familiar not strange. My grandfather was born in Oxenhope and when I studied Mrs Gaskell's *Life of Charlotte Brontë* for my Higher School Certificate I was privileged to know the detail of just what I was studying. I belonged. And my local qualifications, so dear to Yorkshiremen, have influenced my attitudes to the Brontë Society which, like Charles Lemon, I have been honoured to serve.

This book speaks for itself. It deserves to be widely read by new visitors to Haworth who are placing the village on their own maps. The spell holds, and I am sure that like the spell of Brontë novels, poems and pictures, it will hold through the new millenium.

Asa Briggs
Lewes, 1996

Haworth and District OS Map 1852

Haworth Village (part) – Prepared for the General Board of Health 1853

INTRODUCTION

'I still preach once on Sunday . . . We still have a great many calls from Lords and ladies and others, but they do not stop long as I cannot do with much company.'

So wrote Mr Brontë early in February 1859 to his brother Hugh in Ballinaskeagh.

Years later, Mr Nicholls would recall how he protected his father-in-law, on the short journey from the church to the parsonage, from being waylaid by interviewers who pressed forward to clasp the hand of the father of the Brontës.*

In 1884 Mr Brontë's successor, John Wade, wrote** to an American admirer who had paid for the memorial window to Charlotte in the new church: 'I hope it will be possible for you to see the window at some time and we shall be most happy to see you here in what was the home of Charlotte Bronté [*sic*] . . . As thousands of people come here in the course of a year we are obliged for the sake of the privacy of a large family to decline to receive visitors into the house, but we most cordially concede to you the right, in return for your loving regard for Miss Bronté's memory to introduce within the house any person you wish and as many as you wish . . .'

Many visitors had begun arriving at the Parsonage before Charlotte's death. In a letter*** dated 22 February 1850 to W.S. Williams she writes:

> 'I believe both *Shirley* and *Jane Eyre* are being a good deal read in the North just now – but I only hear fitful rumours from time to time – and my life of anchorite seclusion shuts out all bearers of tidings. One or two curiosity-hunters have made their way to Haworth Parsonage – but our rude hills and rugged neighbourhood will I doubt not form a sufficient barrier to the frequent repetition of such visits.'

A few days later Charlotte was writing to Ellen Nussey****:

* From the obituary for the second Mrs Nicholls, published in *The Times* on 2 March 1915.

** Letter dated 23 May 1884 to Thomas Hockley, Philadelphia. (BST 6:22:1920).

*** SHB III 79.

**** SHB III 81.

> 'I scribble you a line in haste to tell you of my proceedings. Various folks are beginning to come boring to Haworth, on the errand of seeing the scenery described in *Jane Eyre* and *Shirley*; amongst others, Sir J.K. Shuttleworth and Lady Shuttleworth have persisted in coming; they were here on Friday.'

As far as is known, the Shuttleworths left no record of this visit and it may be interesting, not to say amusing, to include here the remainder of Charlotte's letter:

> 'The baronet looks in vigorous health, he scarcely appears more than thirty-five, but says he is forty-four; Lady Shuttleworth is rather handsome and still young. They were both quite unpretending, etc. When here they again urged me to visit them. Papa took their side at once, would not hear of my refusing; I must go, this left me without plea or defence. I consented to go for three days, they wanted me to return with them in the carriage, but I pleaded off till to-morrow. I wish it was well over.
>
> If all be well I shall be able to write more about them when I come back. Sir James is very courtly, fine-looking; I wish he may be as sincere as he is polished. He shows his white teeth with too frequent a smile; but I will not prejudge him.'

In his monograph on Charlotte Brontë, published in 1877, Sir Thomas Wemyss Reid observed:

> 'One great change resulted immediately from the publication of Mrs Gaskell's work: Haworth and its parsonage became the shrine to which hundreds of literary pilgrims from all parts of the world began to find their way to see the house in which the three sisters had spent their lives and done their work, to stand at the altar at which Charlotte was married, and beneath which her ashes now rest, and to hear her aged father preach one of his pithy, sensible, but dogmatic sermons, was what all literary lion-hunters aspired to do. In Yorkshire, indeed, the stolid people of the West Riding were not greatly moved by this enthusiasm. Just as Charlotte herself had seemed an ordinary and rather obscure person to her Yorkshire friends, so Haworth was still regarded as being a very dull and dreary village by those who lived near it. But the empire of genius knows no geographical boundaries, and if at her own doors Charlotte Brontë's sway was unrecognised, from far-distant quarters of the world there came the free and full acknowledgement of her power. No other

land, however, furnished so many eager and enthusiastic visitors to the Brontë shrine as the United States, and the number of Americans who found their way to Haworth during the ten years immediately following the death of the author of *Jane Eyre* would, if properly recorded, astonish the world...'

American pilgrims were conspicuous in those early days as it was not long after the publication of the novels that cheap editions became widely available in their country. There were no international copyright laws at that time: *Jane Eyre* and *Wuthering Heights* were published in New York in January and July 1848 respectively by Harper & Brothers. *The Tenant of Wildfell Hall* appeared there in July 1848*.

Towards the end of the century it so happened that Mr Claude Meeker, the U.S. Consul in Bradford, was an enthusiastic supporter of the newly-formed Brontë Society and he was quoted in the *Bradford Telegraph* as saying 'The village of Haworth has many American visitors during the summer months. The home of the Brontës is indeed an honoured shrine with literary Americans and few of them visit this part of the country without inspecting the quaint Yorkshire village.'

After a century and a half the home of the Brontës still attracts many visitors but they do not confine themselves nowadays to coming in the summer months, they are not all literary pilgrims and Haworth is no longer a quaint Yorkshire village.

Early visitors would have been moved to set down their pioneering experiences. Researches in connection with *A Centenary History of the Brontë Society – 1893–1993* brought to light a number of such accounts, mostly long-forgotten, which had appeared in newspapers and periodicals as well as in the *Transactions* of the Brontë Society. The Society's Council has therefore decided that it would be timely to republish a selection of these accounts which are not only informative but of real historical interest. Some, for instance, record meetings with Patrick Brontë, Charlotte and Arthur Nicholls.

It is clear from the pages which follow that there were entrepreneurs in Haworth who early saw commercial possibilities in the growing number of Brontë worshippers coming to Haworth. Among them were John Brown, the sexton (who died in 1855), his brother William (who succeeded him) and John Greenwood, the stationer (who marketed the souvenir stationery on which Charles Hale's letter was written). Between them they started the industry which flourishes in the village to this day.

* See page 27.

A routine developed for those first intrepid souls: staying at the Black Bull was a must, where John Brown, and later his brother, would appear for an introductory talk. A call on Martha Brown followed and thereafter for the fortunate ones a call at the Parsonage. Many visits ended with a moorland walk – not universally enjoyed, especially if the weather was unfavourable. When prevailed upon the aged Mr Brontë received visitors with model kindness. His views on Mrs Gaskell's *Life* appear inconsistent but he can be forgiven, bearing in mind some of the excesses of the first edition. There are mixed reports about Mr Nicholls but in the main his work as a pastor was widely acclaimed and made him a well-loved figure. The few reports of his unpopularity in the pages which follow probably stemmed from Mrs Gaskell who did not get on with him.

It is remarkable how prominently Branwell remained in the memories of his contemporaries. He was, of course, more of a public figure than his sisters, and something of his personality and his exceptional, if unusual, abilities clearly became legendary.

Factual errors will be observed here and there, particularly in those accounts written with hindsight. Ellen Nussey, for example, writing her reminiscences in 1871 for *Scribner's Magazine,* nearly forty years after her first visit to Haworth, describes Mr Brontë, then in his mid-fifties, as having snow white hair. There is also confusion as to the state of Mr Brontë's eyesight.

In the accounts of visitors coming to Haworth having read Mrs Gaskell's *Life*, published in 1857, there is a tendency for a pattern to evolve. Charles Hale in 1861 was actually staying with the Gaskells and sets down from time to time what he has heard from his hostess in person. The facts as he presents them are not always quite correct but it is possible that Mrs Gaskell was sometimes to blame.

PART I

IN THE DAYS OF THE BRONTËS

1

Reminiscences of Charlotte Brontë by Ellen Nussey, 1833

Scribner's Monthly II, May 1871; also Brontë Society *Transactions* II. Pt.X 58

Charlotte Brontë and Ellen Nussey first met at Miss Wooler's Roe Head school in 1831. Their friendship was to be terminated only by Charlotte's death. Thereafter Mrs Gaskell received considerable help from Ellen when writing her *Life of Charlotte Brontë* but many years passed before Ellen could be persuaded to set down her own story which finally appeared in *Scribner's Monthly* in New York in May, 1871, the editor having asked her for some reminiscences of the Brontë family. In the following extract Ellen describes her first visit to Haworth in the summer of 1833:

> . . . My first visit to Haworth was full of novelty and freshness. The scenery for some miles before we reached Haworth was wild and uncultivated, with hardly any population; at last we came to what seemed a terrific hill, such a steep declivity no one thought of riding down it; the horse had to be carefully led. We no sooner reached the foot of this hill than we had to begin to mount again, over a narrow, rough stone-paved road; the horses' feet seemed to catch at boulders, as if climbing. When we reached the top of the village there was apparently no outlet, but we were directed to drive into an entry which just admitted the gig; we wound round in this entry and then saw the church close at hand, and we entered on the short lane which led to the parsonage gateway. Here Charlotte was waiting, having caught the sound of the approaching gig. When greetings and introductions were over, Miss Branwell (the aunt of the Brontës) took possession of their guest and treated her with the care and solicitude due to a weary traveller. Mr Brontë, also, was stirred out of his usual retirement by his

own kind consideration, for not only the guest but the man-servant and the horse were to be made comfortable. He made enquiries about the man, of his length of service, &c., with the kind purpose of making a few moments of conversation agreeable to him.

Even at this time, Mr Brontë struck me as looking very venerable, with his snow-white hair* and powdered coat-collar. His manner and mode of speech always had the tone of high-bred courtesy. He was considered somewhat of an invalid, and always lived in the most abstemious and simple manner. His white cravat was not then so remarkable as it grew to be afterwards. He was in the habit of covering this cravat himself. We never saw the operation, but we always had to wind for him the white sewing-silk which he used. Charlotte said it was her father's one extravagance – he cut up yards and yards of white lutestring (silk) in covering his cravat; and like Dr Joseph Woolffe (the renowned and learned traveller), who, when on a visit and in a long fit of absence, 'went into a clean shirt every day for a week, without taking one off,' so Mr Brontë's cravat went into new silk and new size without taking any off, till at length nearly half his head was enveloped in cravat. His liability to attacks, no doubt, attached him to this increasing growth of cravat.

Miss Branwell was a very small, antiquated little lady. She wore caps large enough for half a dozen of the present fashion, and a front of light auburn curls over her forehead. She always dressed in silk. She had a horror of the climate so far north, and of the stone floors in the parsonage. She amused us by clicking about in pattens** whenever she had to go into the kitchen or look after household operations...

In fine and suitable weather delightful rambles were made over the moors, and down into the glens and ravines that here and there broke the monotony of the moorland. The rugged bank and rippling brook were treasures of delight. Emily, Anne and Branwell used to ford the streams, and sometimes placed stepping-stones for the other two; there was always a lingering delight in these spots – every moss, every flower, every tint and form, were noted and enjoyed. Emily especially had a gleesome delight in these nooks of beauty – her reserve for the time vanished. One long ramble made in these early days was far away over the moors to a spot familiar to Emily and Anne, which

* Writing here from memory in 1871 Ellen Nussey describes Mr Brontë's hair in 1833 as snow white; in 1850 it is described as nearly white (see p. 10). Hair samples at the parsonage vary from auburn shot through with white to pure white.

** Wooden overshoes. Now in BPM.

they called 'The Meeting of the Waters'. It was a small oasis of emerald green turf, broken here and there by small clear springs; a few large stones served as resting-spaces; seated here, we were hidden from all the world, nothing appearing in view but miles and miles of heather, a glorious blue sky, and brightening sun. A fresh breeze wafted on us its exhilarating influence: we laughed and made mirth of each other, and settled we would call ourselves the quartette. Emily, half reclining on a slab of stone, played like a young child with the tadpoles in the water, making them swim about, and then fell to moralizing on the strong and the weak, the brave and the cowardly, as she chased them with her hand. No serious care or sorrow had so far cast its gloom on nature's youth and buoyancy, and nature's simplest offerings were fountains of pleasure and enjoyment.

The interior of the now far-famed parsonage lacked drapery of all kinds. Mr Brontë's horror of fire forbade curtains to the windows; they never had these accessories to comfort and appearance till long after Charlotte was the only inmate of the family sitting-room, – she then ventured on the innovation when her friend was with her; it did not please her father, but it was not forbidden.

There was not much carpet anywhere except in the dining-room, and on the study floor. The hall floor and stairs were done with sand-stone, always beautifully clean, as everything was about the house; the walls were not papered but stained in a pretty dove-coloured tint; hair-seated chairs and mahogany tables, book-shelves in the study, but not many of these elsewhere. Scant and bare indeed, many will say, yet it was not a scantness that made itself felt. Mind and thought, I had almost said elegance, but certainly refinement, diffused themselves over all, and made nothing really wanting.

A little later on, there was the addition of a piano.* Emily, after some application, played with precision and brilliancy. Anne played also, but she preferred soft harmonies and vocal music. She sang a little; her voice was weak, but very sweet in tone.

Mr Brontë's health caused him to retire early. He assembled his household for family worship at eight o'clock; at nine he locked and barred the front door, always giving as he passed the sitting-room a kindly admonition to the 'children' not to be late; half-way up the stairs he stayed his steps to wind up the clock ... Every morning was heard the firing of a pistol from Mr Brontë's room window, – it was

* It is still in Mr Brontë's study.

the discharging of the loading which was made every night. Mr Brontë's tastes led him to delight in the perusal of battle-scenes, and in following the artifice of war; had he entered on military service instead of ecclesiastical he would probably have had a very distinguished career...

The services in church in these days were such as can only be seen (if ever seen again) in localities like Haworth. The people assembled, but it was apparently to *listen*. Any part beyond that was quite out of their reckoning. All through the prayers, a stolid look of apathy was fixed on the generality of their faces. There they sat, or leaned, in their pews; some few, perhaps, were resting, after a long walk over the moors. The children, many of them in clogs (or sabots), pattered in from school after service had commenced, and pattered out again before the sermon. The sexton, with a long staff, continually walked round in the aisles, 'knobbing' sleepers when he dare, shaking his head at and threatening unruly children; but when the sermon began there was a change. Attitudes took the listening forms. Mr Brontë always addressed his hearers in extempore style. Very often he selected a parable from one of the Gospels, which he explained in the simplest manner – sometimes going over his own words and explaining them so as to be perfectly intelligible to the lowest comprehension...

Haworth of the present day, like many other secluded places, has made a step onwards, in that it has now its railway station and its institutions for the easy acquirement of learning, politics, and literature. The parsonage is quite another habitation from the parsonage of former days. The garden, which was nearly all grass, and possessed only a few stunted thorns and shrubs, and a few currant bushes which Emily and Anne treasured as their own bit of fruit-garden, is now a perfect Arcadia of floral culture and beauty...

2

John Stores Smith's Day with Charlotte Brontë in 1850

by Professor Kathleen Tillotson,
Brontë Society *Transactions* 16. Pt 1. 22 (1971)

This account by John Stores Smith was published in a Manchester literary weekly, the *Free Lance*, in 1868 and what follows is based on a contribution to *Transactions* by Professor Kathleen Tillotson.

John Stores Smith, who lived in Manchester, was only 22 at the time of his visit but had already published three books, including a biography of Mirabeau. In pursuance of a literary career he later moved to London but after a few months the venture failed and he returned to Manchester to re-enter the world of commerce.

In 1850 he belonged to a small coterie in Halifax of enthusiastic lovers of literature. When he joined them they had all read Currer Bell's novels and it was rumoured locally that they were from the pen of a lady, living only nine miles away across the moors.

It was resolved that Smith should 'help fate a little' by sending her a presentation copy of his *Mirabeau* (published in 1848). His communication was 'boldly addressed to Miss Brontë'; its acknowledgment was signed by Currer Bell. His account continues:

> For Currer Bell to acknowledge by return of post the receipt of a letter addressed to Miss Brontë placed their identity beyond a doubt; and many Sundays had not elapsed before two of our party were seized with an ardent desire to attend Divine service at the Parish Church of Haworth. I was not of the two. Rising betimes they crossed the moors, and reached the place in time for morning service, and when it was over they left the church, and, ostensibly studying epitaphs, placed themselves in such a position as to command a sight of anyone

coming from the church to the Parsonage. They were gratified by the vision of a lady who perfectly realised their preconceived idea of Currer Bell, and who, it subsequently was made manifest, was *not* Miss Brontë. But we were not the less deeply interested with their graphic account of the place and the personal appearance of our supposed authoress . . .

A further correspondence ensued ending with an invitation to dinner. Stores Smith continues:

I found myself at the Keighley station on a lovely morning in September, and I was, I believe, the first person out of her own immediate circle of relatives and friends who spent a day with Charlotte Brontë in her own home, now familiar by pen and pencil to everyone to whom genius is admirable and the tragedies of domestic life are sacred . . .

The parsonage was a low stone house, which occupied one corner of the graveyard. A field had evidently been set apart, and the founders of the church had said: 'In three-fourths of it we will inter the dead, and in that other fourth we will bury the living.' A little garden was before it, and you stepped straight off the gravestones into it. You also went down one step, as towards a larger grave. A flagged walk led up to the front door, and it was covered over with a damp, green film, and in the interstices grew an almost black moss. The garden on either side was filled with various common country plants and shrubs, but bore no trace of any care or attention, and the exuberant vegetation of autumn's excess hid their nature, and gave me the phantom-like feeling that I was looking upon the colony of the fabled Mandrake. The stone of the house was of the same melancholy tint as the flags of the walk; a small door was in the centre, and a window on either side; in the only storey above were three windows [*sic*] I think. Of all the sad, heart-broken looking dwellings I had passed through this looked the saddest. A great sinking of spirit came over me, and I wished I had not come. I felt that my face, could I have seen it, had instinctively put on that expression of the place. What was I doing taking the hot blood and rollicking high spirits of one-and-twenty into this silent and sombre catacomb? . . .

At this instant the door opened and the servant appeared, and behind her on the stairs, the authoress of *Jane Eyre*. Here was a romantic meeting. An enthusiastic genius-lover and hero-worshipper, with a heart aflame towards literature, and all its priests and sybils, literally

Ambrotype of Haworth Parsonage, c. 1855–1859. Three steps lead up to the front door. Today there are seven. See *Haworth Parsonage: The Home of the Brontës*, 1977, by Jocelyn Kellett, p. 26.

blazing with earnestness, makes a pilgrimage to the most original lady of the age . . .

To this hour I have only a confused recollection of a slender lady, more like a spirit than a corporeal being, bidding me welcome, with a quiet, amused smile on her lips; of her telling me that she had half-an-hour's writing that must be done ere dinner, and, having asked me to be so good as to pass that interval with her father, of her opening a door to the right and showing me into a small room, and with the words 'Father, this is Mr Smith whom I have told you about', closing the door behind me, and leaving me flustered and confused in the presence of a blind old man. Had I never seen more of Miss Brontë, I should have had no impression of her left upon my mind.

The Reverend Mr Brontë was the ruin of what had been a striking and singularly handsome man. He was tall, strongly built, and even then perfectly erect. His hair was nearly white, but his eyebrows were still black; his features were large and handsome, but he was quite blind.* He was dressed very carelessly, in almost worn out clothes, had no proper necktie, and was in slippers. He sat beside the fire place erect in his chair, facing the window, and he seemed to look steadfastly towards the light with his sightless orbs, which were never again to behold it, until the celestial splendour of the New Jerusalem flash upon them, when sun and moon and stars shall be no more. The blind dog** curled himself on the hearth at his blind old master's feet. He commenced conversation almost immediately upon his daughter. I had read and admired her works? I told him I had, and gave my honest opinion of their fascinating interest and startling originality. And was that the general verdict of the world? I gave him a summary of many criticisms I well remembered, and at every pause he rubbed his knees slowly and muttered in half-soliloquy: 'And I hadn't an idea of it. To think of me never even suspecting it. Strange! Strange!' And then he talked about Emily and the other sister and told me how he had considered Emily the genius of his family, how he never fancied Charlotte capable of writing anything and could scarcely realise it; and as he did so, he ever and anon fell into reverie again and muttered the old refrain 'And I knew nothing about it, positively nothing. Strange! Perhaps I might have stopped it if I had. But I knew nothing – nothing.' He seemed to have a threefold feeling; regret that novels should have proceeded from his daughters; paternal pride, evident and sometimes garrulously demonstrative pride; and a wandering inability altogether to believe it. After a little while he turned upon the untimely deaths of his younger children, dwelt much upon both, and then fell into soliloquy once more: 'And she is dead! And Emily dead too! Both dead! All dead !'

How could I talk to him? What were my inflated schemes and random day dreams, what was the weather, or trade, or politics, to this blind old ruin sitting there, confused amid the splendour of his child's success, and mourning on the sad hearth-stone of a bereaved fire-side? I could not talk. I could only sit subdued and depressed, as I might have kept watch beside a corpse. For the first time in my life I had practical experience that even in the comet-like track of genius all is not brilliance. Here

* Not so at this time. Four years had elapsed since Mr Brontë's reasonably successful cataract operation.

** Keeper, who died in December 1851.

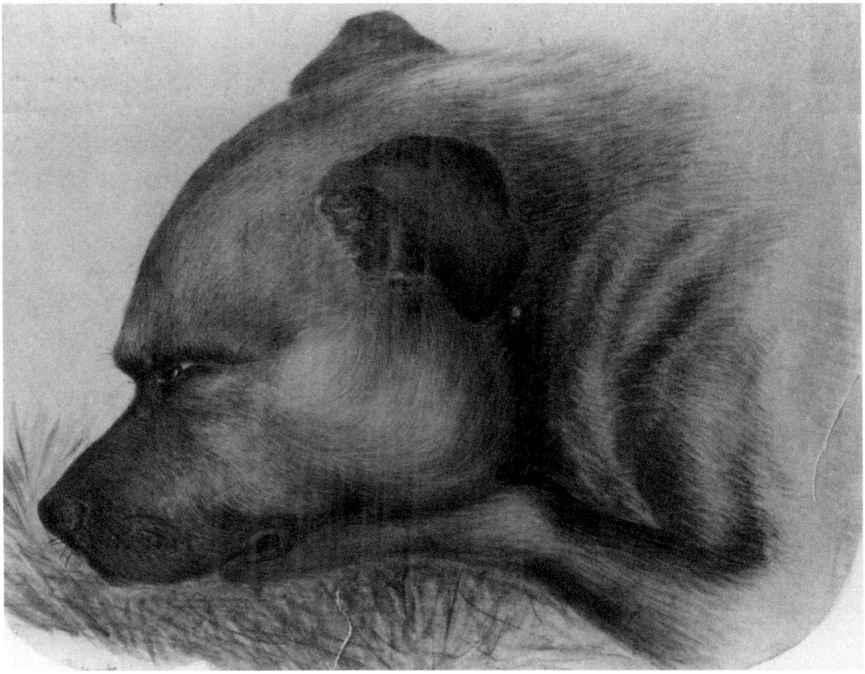

Keeper. Water colour by Emily Brontë. Titled, dated and signed in ink, 24 April 1838.

was the most original living Englishwoman, who had broken out into the full glory of an achieved success, whose pen was wealth to her, whose name was on every cultivated tongue, and whose creations were in every cultivated mind, and this – this was her home!

I was so musing when, after the lapse of about an hour, the door opened and the servant announced dinner.

I was shown across the lobby into the parlour to the left, and there I found Miss Brontë, standing in the full light of the window, and I had ample opportunity of fixing her upon my memory, where her image is vividly present to this hour. She was diminutive in height, and extremely fragile in figure. Her hand was one of the smallest I have ever grasped. She had no pretensions to being considered beautiful, and was as far removed from being plain. She had rather light brown hair, somewhat thin, and drawn plainly over her brow. Her complexion had no trace of colour in it, and her lips were pallid also but she had a most sweet smile with a touch of tender melancholy in it. Altogether she was as unpretending, undemonstrative, quiet a little lady as you could well meet. Her age I took to be about five-and-thirty. But when you saw and felt her eyes, the spirit that created *Jane Eyre* was revealed at once to you. They were rather small, but of a very peculiar colour, and had a strange lustre and intensity. They were chameleon-like, a blending of various brown and olive tints. But they looked you through and through – and you felt they were forming an opinion of you, not by mere noting of Lavaterish* physiognomical peculiarities, but by a subtle penetration into the very marrow of your mind, and the innermost core of your soul. Taking my hand again she apologised for her enforced absence, and, as she did so, she looked right through me. There was no boldness in the gaze, but an intense, direct, searching look, as of one who had the gift to read hidden mysteries, and the right to read them. I had a feeling that I never experienced before or since, as though I was being mesmerised. It was almost a relief when the look was removed, and we sat down together to table. During dinner I had always a feeling that those eyes were on me, when I was looking down myself, and when I looked at her, and her gaze was on her plate, I could still not divest myself of the sensation that those eyes could see one through their lids. We did not converse much while the simple meal was being dispatched, but afterward we had a ceaseless talk extending over fully two hours. I have not one single phrase of her conversation to chronicle. There was neither wit, nor fancy, nor brilliance in her remarks. Her talk was remarkable for strong, shrewd, homely sense; tersely, briefly, directly and vigorously expressed. There was not a trace of the literary woman about her. No attempt at effect, no *tours de phrase*. The merit of her remarks lay altogether in the matter and not the least in the manner. About herself and sisters, and family generally, she was reticent, and seemed to put the subject markedly away from her. She confined her observations to myself, my designs and prospects, and to the expression of her views of London literary men and their lives and characters.

As regards myself, she at once assumed an almost maternal tone. I was then about to perpetrate one of those colossal follies which only

* Johann Lavater (1741–1801) founder of physiognomy, the science of analysing the contours of the skull to determine a person's dispositions, characteristics and talents. Its phrenological theories long ago gave way to more scientific methods. Charlotte Brontë and George Smith visited a London phrenologist anonymously in June 1851. The subsequent estimate relating to Charlotte is in the BPM. She uses the word 'physiognomy' three times in *Shirley*. The relevant entry in the Shorter Oxford Dictionary quotes her further use of the word in *Villette* Chapter VII.

the fervour of youth renders possible; which we lament for many years, and then, later in life, envy the heart that was capable of such courageous, hopeful recklessness. I was about to abandon reliable commerce, and go up to London and take my chance in the intricate jungle of literature. She did not directly endeavour to dissuade me. I fancy those mesmeric eyes had told her that that would be as hopeless a task as to attempt to make Haworth lively. But she did point out that if I continued to write such matter as, she was complimentary enough to say, was alone worthy of me, I must starve, and she seemed to think the tamest Haworth life was preferable to the turning of the pen into a literary tight-rope-dancing machine for gold. But she sought to turn me away from London by an indirect method. Whether she exaggerated her real sentiments for my benefit, or whether she afterwards in any way modified her views, I do not know, but certainly in 1850, shortly after her visit to London as a literary lioness, she pictured her impressions of metropolitan literary life in most forbidding colours, and with clear, cutting intense distaste of it; I may even say contempt. Dickens she had met [not elsewhere recorded] and admired his genius, but did not like him. Her homely thrift, and unpretending, retiring nature, shrank from him, from an idea she had acquired of ostentatious extravagance on his part. Thackeray she absolutely worshipped. Carlyle she knew little of, but reverenced the dignity of his life, though she disliked his writings. Of one eminent man in criticism, and metaphysical and scientific literature [presumably G. H. Lewes] she had an absolute loathing; and of the ruck and run of the minor Guerillas and Bohemians of Letters she spoke with a supreme contempt. She had looked literary life full in the face, and was contented to die in Haworth, rather than to live in that. Throughout all this she evinced an almost tender interest in myself the sincerity of which it was impossible to doubt, and the effect of which did not fail to be pleasing and affecting. She evidently said to herself, Here is an ingenuous youth, with the sails of his fresh manhood full set and the colours of an exalted imagination flying, bearing straight down upon Charybdis; I will strain my graphic power to show him clearly that it is to Charybdis he is going. I remember well her last words. They were: 'When you get to London, seek out and gain the friendship of the highest and best in literature, and them only. Try to get the acquaintance of Mr Thackeray, maintain that of Mr Carlyle; but as for the general body of those who call themselves literary men avoid them as a moral pestilence.'

By this time it was five o'clock, and I took my leave. I left by the back way. I strode away through the long street of Haworth and mounted the eastward hills; and it was not until the fresh breezes of the moors were blowing over me that I felt the sense of despondent depression in any way lightened. As it was I turned round and bade adieu to the receding church and parsonage with feelings of pain and sorrow. I was sorry for the solitary lady I had left behind. I never dreamed she would have married, but I felt that she must die. I was sorry for myself. I felt that I had met a Cassandra, and though my will was determined not to heed her, the still small voice within me said that her vaticinations were correct, and that I was on my way to disaster. Both feelings were correct. I encountered shipwreck and Miss Brontë died.

So ended my day with Charlotte Brontë. A more unrelieved oppressive story than her's and her sisters' I do not recollect. Their brief existence was one overclouding nightmare, and the hand that touched them and dispelled it was the hand of death.

In conclusion Professor Tillotson remarked that in spite of Smith's errors and occasional journalistic embroideries of fact, and the slight suspicion attaching to any uncorroborated post-Gaskell reminiscence, his account seemed to her substantially authentic; in his representation of Charlotte's views on London literary life there is more than he could have gleaned from the *Life* and it is clearly related to his own subsequent experiences.

Professor Tillotson has since kindly pointed out that correspondence included in Vol.6 of the *Letters of Charles Dickens*, published by the Clarendon Press in 1988, makes it clear that in 1850 Dickens narrowly missed meeting Charlotte Brontë at the home of George Smith. She stayed with the Smiths from 30 May until 25 June that year and Dickens was invited by them to dinner on 7 June but was unable to accept on account of 'other and less agreeable engagements' (p. 110). Earlier Charlotte had hoped to see him at the Anniversary Dinner of the Royal Literary Fund on 15 May but was obliged to postpone her London visit owing to her father's illness.

3

Letter from Bessie Parkes to Elizabeth Gaskell, October 1850

Shakespeare Head Brontë III 167

Some days after Stores Smith there came another visitor who was moved to write of her experience in a letter dated 3 October 1850 to her friend Elizabeth Gaskell. Bessie Parkes (1829–1925) was the daughter of a Unitarian radical lawyer, who was also a Birmingham M.P. and a friend of the Brownings, George Eliot and the Gaskells. She became a prominent feminist and in 1850 toured Europe unchaperoned with a woman friend.

At the death of the Duke of Wellington in 1852 she was invited by a Hastings newspaper to report on the funeral. This was her first assignment which convinced her that journalism was her true vocation. In 1858 she acquired a small paper which was adapted to produce *The English Woman's Journal*. This she edited for four years until ill-health obliged her to give up and the paper ceased publication two years later. She also became a minor writer of her day and subsequently published a pamphlet *Remarks on the Education of Girls* which was severely attacked. She was widowed early in her married life and left with two children, one of whom was Hilaire Belloc, the poet and writer.

Bessie Parkes was twenty years old when she wrote to Mrs Gaskell. To a young girl the Parsonage might have seemed depressing, but she wisely assumes that cheerfulness and hope could at times have abounded within its walls:

> Though the weather was drizzly we resolved to make our long-planned excursion to Haworth; so we packed ourselves into the buffalo skin, and that into the gig, and set off about eleven. The rain ceased, and the day was just suited to the scenery – wild and chill – with great masses of cloud glooming over the moors, and here and there a ray of sunshine

covertly stealing through, and resting with a dim magical light upon some high bleak village; or darting down into some deep glen, lighting the tall chimney, or glistening on the windows and wet roof of the mill which lies couching in the bottom.

The country got wilder and wilder as we approached Haworth; for the last four miles we were ascending a huge moor, at the very top of which lies the dreary, black-looking village of Haworth. The village street itself is one of the steepest hills I have ever seen, and the stones are so horribly jolting that I should have got out and walked with W---, if possible, but having once begun the ascent, to stop was out of the question. At the top was the inn where we put up, close by the church; and the clergyman's house, we were told, was at the top of the churchyard. So through that we went – a dreary, dreary place, literally *paved* with rain-blackened tombstones, and all on the slope; for at Haworth there is on the highest height a higher still, and Mr Brontë's house stands considerably above the church. There was the house before us, a small oblong stone house, with not a tree to screen it from the cutting wind; but how we were to get at it from the churchyard we could not see!

There was an old man in the churchyard, brooding like a ghoul over the graves, with a sort of grim hilarity on his face. I thought he looked hardly human; however, he was human enough to tell us the way, and presently we found ourselves in the little bare parlour. Presently the door opened, and in came a superannuated mastiff, followed by an old gentleman very like Miss Brontë who shook hands with us, and then went to call his daughter. A long interval, during which we coaxed the old dog, and looked at a picture of Miss Brontë, by Richmond, the solitary ornament of the room, looking strangely out of place on the bare walls, and at the books on the little shelves, most of them evidently the gift of the authors since Miss Brontë's celebrity. Presently she came in, and welcomed us very kindly, and took me upstairs to take off my bonnet, and herself brought water and towels. The uncarpeted stone stairs and floors, the old drawers propped on wood, were all scrupulously clean and neat.

When we went into the parlour again we began talking very comfortably, when the door opened and Mr Brontë looked in; seeing his daughter there, I suppose he thought it was all right, and he retreated to his study on the opposite side of the passage, presently emerging again to bring W--- a country newspaper. This was his last appearance till we went. Miss Brontë spoke with the greatest warmth

Flossy. Watercolour by Emily Brontë c. 1843.

of Miss Martineau,* and of the good she had gained from her. Well! We talked about various things – the character of the people, about her solitude, etc. – till she left the room to help about dinner, I suppose, for she did not return for an age. The old dog had vanished; a fat curly-haired dog** honoured us with her company for some time, but finally manifested a wish to get out, so we were left alone. At last Miss Brontë returned, followed by the maid and dinner, which made us all more comfortable; and we had some very pleasant conversation, in the midst of which time passed quicker than we supposed, for at last W––– found that it was half-past three, and we had fourteen or fifteen miles before us. So we hurried off, having obtained from her a promise to pay us a visit in the spring; and the old gentleman having issued once more from his study to say good-bye, we returned to the inn, and made the best of our way homewards.

Miss Brontë put me so in mind of her own Jane Eyre. She looked smaller than ever, and moved about so quietly, and noiselessly, just

* A breach occurred later between the two ladies following Miss Martineau's adverse criticism of *Villette*.

** Flossy. See also page 120.

like a little bird, as Rochester called her, barring that all birds are joyous, and that joy can never have entered that house since it was first built; and yet, perhaps, when that old man married, and took home his bride, and children's voices and feet were heard about the house, even that desolate crowded graveyard and biting blast could not quench cheerfulness and hope. Now there is something touching in the sight of that little creature entombed in such a place, and moving about herself like a spirit, especially when you think that the slight still frame encloses a force of strong fiery life, which nothing has been able to freeze or extinguish.

4

Letter from Elizabeth Gaskell to an unknown correspondent, September 1853

The Life of Charlotte Brontë, 1857, Vol. II, Chapter XIII

The letter from Bessie Parkes would have greatly interested Elizabeth Gaskell who had met Charlotte for the first time in August 1850 at the home of Sir James Kay-Shuttleworth at Briery Close, Windermere, but her first visit to Haworth did not take place until the end of September 1853 when the weather appears to have been similar to that experienced by Bessie Parkes. Mrs Gaskell described the visit in a letter to an unknown correspondent and later included it in her biography:

> It was a dull, drizzly, India-inky day, all the way on the railroad to Keighley, which is a rising wool manufacturing town, lying in a hollow between hills – not a pretty hollow, but more what the Yorkshire people call a 'bottom' or 'botham'. I left Keighley in a car for Haworth, four miles off- four tough, steep scrambling miles, the road winding between wave-like hills, that rose and fell on every side of the horizon, with a long illimitable sinuous look, as if they were part of the line of the Great Serpent, which the Norse legend says, girdles the world. The day was lead-coloured; the road had stone factories alongside of it, – grey, dull-coloured rows of stone cottages belonging to these factories; – and then we came to poor, hungry-looking fields, – stone-fences everywhere, and trees nowhere. Haworth is a long straggling village: one steep narrow street – so steep that the flagstones with which it is paved are placed end-ways that the horses' feet may have something to cling to, and not slip down backwards; which if they did, they would soon reach Keighley. But if the horses had cats' feet and claws, they would do all the better. Well, we (the man, horse, car, and I) clambered up this street, and reached the Church; then we

Charlotte Brontë. Portrait in chalk by George Richmond, 1850 (National Portrait Gallery).

turned off into a lane on the left, past the curate's lodging in the Sexton's, past the School-house, up to the Parsonage yard-door. I went round the house to the front door, looking to the church; moors everywhere beyond and above. The crowded grave-yard surrounds the house, and small grass enclosure for drying clothes.

I don't know that I ever saw a spot more exquisitely clean; the most dainty place for that I ever saw. To be sure, the life is like clock-work. No one comes to the house; you catch the ticking of the clock in the kitchen, or the buzzing of a fly in the parlour, all over the house. Miss Brontë sits alone in her parlour; breakfasting with her father in his study at nine o'clock. She helps in the housework; for one of their servants, Tabby, is nearly eighty, and the other only a girl. Then I accompanied her in her walks on the sweeping moors; the heather-bloom had been blighted by a thunder-storm a day or two before, and was all of a livid brown colour, instead of the blaze of purple glory it ought to have been.* Oh! those high, wild, desolate moors, up above the whole world, and the very realms of silence! Home to dinner at two. Mr Brontë has his dinner sent in to him. All the small table arrangements had the same dainty simplicity about them. Then we rested, and talked, over the clear bright fire; it is a cold country, and the fires were a pretty warm dancing light all over the house. The parlour has been evidently refurnished within the last few years, since Miss Brontë's success has enabled her to have a little more money to spend. Everything fits into, and is in harmony with the idea of a country parsonage, possessed by people of very moderate means. The prevailing colour of the room is crimson, to make a warm setting for the cold grey landscape without. There is her likeness by Richmond;** and an engraving from Lawrence's picture of Thackeray; and two recesses, on each side of the high, narrow old-fashioned mantel-piece, filled with books, – books given to her, books she has bought, and which tell of her individual pursuits and tastes; *not* standard books.

She cannot see well, and does little beside knitting. The way she weakened her eyesight was this: when she was 16 or 17, she wanted much to *draw*; and she copied niminipimini copper-plate engravings out of annuals ('stippling,' don't the artists call it?) every little point put in, till at the end of six months she had produced an exquisitely faithful copy of the engraving. She wanted to learn to express her

* This is an unlikely explanation. By the end of September the heather would have begun to fade.

** Sent by George Smith to Mr Brontë in July 1850 and is now in the National Portrait Gallery. A copy hangs in the parlour at the parsonage. At the same time Smith sent Charlotte a portrait of the Duke of Wellington (see page 38). The engraving of Samuel Lawrence's portrait of Thackeray was also a gift from Smith to Charlotte in 1853. Both gifts still hang on the parlour walls.

William Makepeace Thackeray. 'At a late hour yesterday evening I had the honour of receiving at Haworth Parsonage a distinguished guest – none other than W. M. Thackeray Esq. Mindful of the rites of hospitality – I hung him in state this morning. He looks superb in his beautiful, tasteful, gilded gibbet.'

Charlotte Brontë in a letter to George Smith dated 26 February 1853

ideas by drawing. After she had tried to *draw* stories, and not succeeded, she took the better mode of writing; but in so small a hand that it is almost impossible to decipher what she wrote at this time.

But now to return to our quiet hour of rest after dinner. I soon observed that her habits of order were such that she could not go on with the conversation, if a chair was out of its place; everything was arranged with delicate regularity. We talked over the old times of her childhood; of her elder sister's (Maria's) death – just like that of Helen Burns in *Jane Eyre*; of those strange starved days at school; of the desire (almost amounting to illness) of expressing herself in some way, – writing or drawing; of her weakened eyesight, which prevented her doing anything for two years, from the age of 17 to 19; of her being a governess; of her going to Brussels; whereupon I said I disliked Lucy Snowe, and we discussed M. Paul Emanuel; and I told her of –––'s

Branwell Brontë's Pillar Portrait, c. 1834 (National Portrait Gallery). 'The picture was divided, almost in the middle by a great pillar'.

Elizabeth Gaskell, The Life of Charlotte Brontë, Vol. I, Chapter VII

admiration of *Shirley*, which pleased her, for the character of Shirley was meant for her sister Emily, about whom she is never tired of talking, nor I of listening. Emily must have been a remnant of the Titans, – great grand-daughter of the giants, who used to inhabit earth. One day, Miss Brontë brought down a rough, common-looking oil-painting,* done by her brother, of herself, – a little, rather prim-looking girl of eighteen, – and the two other sisters, girls of 16 and 14, with cropped hair, and sad, dreamy-looking eyes... Emily had a

* The Pillar portrait.

great dog, – half mastiff, half bull-dog – so savage etc... This dog went to her funeral, walking side-by-side with her father, and then, to the day of its death, it slept at her room door, snuffing under it, and whining every morning.

We have generally had another walk before tea, which is at six; at half past eight, prayers, and by nine all the household are in bed, except ourselves. We sit up together till ten, or past; and after I go, I hear Miss Brontë come down and walk up and down the room for an hour or so.

5

Reminiscences of the Brontës by Abraham Holroyd, 1853

Thornton and the Brontës by William Scruton, p. 111–114 (John Dale & Co., Ltd., Bradford, 1898)

Abraham Holroyd was a poet, antiquary and historian, who lived at Clayton, near Thornton, but he spent many years in America. He had returned home by 1853 and one Sunday in the summer of that year he met Charlotte at Haworth Church. Years later he wrote an account of his day at Haworth for inclusion in *Thornton and the Brontës* by his friend William Scruton. Holroyd's reference to the cheap editions of Charlotte's novels which he had read and sold in New Orleans confirms why American readership started early and expanded so rapidly:

> ... The Brontës left Thornton when I was only five years old, and of course I knew little of them at the time they lived there... As to Miss Brontë I never saw her to speak to but once. It was in the summer of 1853. I had some time before returned from a sixteen years' absence from home, and, while residing in the southern part of the United States I met with and read her *Jane Eyre* and *Shirley*. So, led by curiosity, I one Sunday went to Haworth, with the desire to see the author of such remarkable works. I was late in arriving at the church, and found a pale young man reading the morning service – I think it was Mr G. de Renzy. Mr Brontë was also in the pulpit, for I knew him at once, having seen him before during my boyhood at Thornton Church. The sexton, Mr Brown, had given me a very good place for seeing every one in the lower part of the church, and during the singing of the hymn before the sermon my eyes wandered off in search of the person I had come to see Face after face I scanned, until at length, in a large square pew near the communion-table and under the organ, I

John Brown (1804–1855)
Sexton at Haworth 1835–1855

William Brown (1807–1876)
Sexton at Haworth 1855–1875

Portraits in oils by Branwell Bronte.

saw Jane Eyre, or rather, I should say, Charlotte Brontë. I had not a doubt of it, for there was not such another face in the whole church ... There was great breadth and volume in her forehead; some resemblance to the portraits of Miss Harriet Martineau, I thought, might also be traced. The cheek-bones appeared to me rather prominent, but the entire face gave me the idea that she had much goodness and gentleness of disposition, and possibly great power over those with whom she might come in contact. Her dress was very plain. It was a gown without any flounce, and had plain narrow sleeves. Over her shoulders was thrown a velvet cape – also very plain. Her bonnet was neat in appearance, but not in the fashion. I had scarcely finished these reflections ere Mr Brontë came in from the vestry. Having given out his text he delivered an extempore sermon, devoid of all oratorical display, and remarkable for studied simplicity. He spoke to his hearers of the hollowness of all earthly pleasures, the uncertainty and brevity of human life, and advised every one to seek religion, and therein, he assured them, they would find 'that peace of God which passeth all understanding.'

At the close of the service I left the church, scarcely knowing which most to admire, 'the old man eloquent,' or his gifted and industrious daughter. I noticed that she did not leave the church until all the congregation were gone; and I was told that it was her invariable custom to wait to the last. I was determined, if possible, to speak to her, and as I had been told she always came out at the back door of the church, I waited there. Everyone had left before she came out, and I then told her the object of my visit. It was to present to the author of *Jane Eyre* a copy of the Common Prayer Book used in the Episcopal Churches in the United States of America. It was a beautifully bound copy, printed in Philadelphia. I told her that I had read and also sold numbers of her books in New Orleans, printed by the Harpers, of New York, costing only about one shilling each (25 cents). She asked me if I had brought copies home with me, but I told her I had not, as the Customs' Officers would have taken them from me at Liverpool. She admired the Prayer Book, and thanked me for it, and said the Harpers of New York had never either written to her or sent her any copies of these books of hers, of which they had sold tens of thousands. As we walked together up the lane to the door of the parsonage, she plied me hard with questions, to all of which I replied, and she seemed much pleased. She also asked me where I was going to stay until my return home, and I told her at Mr Ben Ratcliffe's, when she said she was glad, as they were great friends of hers. We then parted by shaking hands, and I never saw her again.

6

A Pilgrimage to Haworth

The Bradford Observer, 30 April 1857

Contributed

The following account is a good example of the rapid growth of interest in Haworth following the publication of Mrs Gaskell's *Life* on 23 March 1857. Within days our unknown visitors set out from Bradford on foot; thereafter the account is written, with its references to Mrs Gaskell, in time to appear in print little more than a month later.

It starts with a chilling description of the effect on the environment of industrial Bradford but quickly moves on to the pleasanter conditions the travellers experience as they proceed westwards along what is now the B6144 road to Haworth. Their route can be easily traced on the current Ordnance Survey map.

Among the thousands who are around us, comparatively few have traversed the country, or know aught of the obscure spot where Charlotte Brontë spent the best portion of her life, but it is likely now to become famous from the graphic interest that Mrs Gaskell's clever pen has thrown around the fate of her heroine. To approach Haworth from any direction is a task of some difficulty, but the easiest route from Bradford is by rail to Keighley, and thence four miles of a gradually ascending road brings the visitor to the foot of Haworth town, which is comprised in one long street, rising at an angle of almost forty-five degrees.

Leaving Manningham* at an early hour, on one of the late fine mornings, we chose to walk, taking the footpath to Daisy-hill, where we paused to view the varied and extensive prospects from that

* A district of Bradford to the north-west.

The industrial West Riding in the mid-nineteenth century; Bradford from the south-east. From *The History of Bradford* by John James 1841.

elevated summit. Blue hills and dark woods are in the distance, and valleys around, while, as a contrast to the pure morning air, and the radiant face of the smiling country, gladdened with the songs of birds, and illumined by the glorious sunshine, black Bradford far below fumes and puffs its volumes of everlasting smoke, causing us involuntarily to hasten onwards, and be rid for at least one day of soot, smoke and business. Looking in at Chellow Dean Reservoir, with its two beautiful lakes, embosomed in trees, and which, *en passant*, is far less frequented than its beautiful site warrants, we entered the Haworth Road at Sandy Lane Bottom, premising that this is the first valley into which we descend. To the right is Cottingley Moor, alive with busy labourers, who are fast converting that barren tract into arable land. It is tedious and expensive operation, the untilled ground being studded with stones and loose debris. We gladly note the reclamation of these unwholesome tracts to better uses, more especially when we perceive that the more early reclaimed land, covered with a bright green mantle, already gives promise to the husbandman.

A steep ascent, and the stone-fenced region around Wilsden opens to view, the dark colour of the walls giving a sombre aspect to the countryside, relieved, however, on the north by the park and woods around Harden Grange, the beautiful residence of W. B. Ferrand Esq.,* which peeps out from among the trees. Were it not for the variety imparted by the surrounding hills, this is certainly the most cheerless portion of the road. One valuable requisite, however, in the locality is a plentiful supply of pure water, which is admirably filtered by the sandy substratum of the district. Wilsden Church's neat structure is passed to the right, and the road leaves it with an easy ascent. Denholme Church, and the country around it, bleaker in appearance even than the road we traverse, is to the left, bounded by the high lands of Queensbury and Thornton Heights.

A sharp turn, and the Hewenden Valley, with its picturesque reservoir and brawling beck, lies below, the road rapidly descending, but it rises as quickly on the opposite side of the narrow valley. We were gratified on gaining the summit of the road by the cheerful aspect of Cullingworth, which has a thriving appearance, and is enlivened by a handsome church and schools, and a commodious modern mansion located in a beautiful little park. The road hence continues to ascend to Flappitt Springs, a spot much resorted to in summer by invalids, the good air and pure water of the neighbourhood being very efficacious for those who are delicate in health. The views are extensive and beautiful, spreading over a wide extent of the country. Looking back, – Hope-hill, on the left, Wrose-hill, to the right, and Billing-hill, at Rawden, in the background, form a triangle, while, peeping over Hewenden, are seen the pinnacles of Wilsden Church. The intervening country is diversified, the cultivated land driving the moors further away, and, judging from the care and trouble which is bestowed on the land, there seems to be a determination on the part of the cultivators to make the best of the sterile tracts which they are endeavouring to render subservient to the use of mankind.

A short distance from Flappitt a moor is crossed, when suddenly bursts upon the sight a deep and extensive valley, guarded by Haworth at one end, clear and well defined, while Keighley, enshrouded in smoke, lies at the northern extremity. The four miles of country between the towns is dotted with all kinds and sizes of residences,

* William Busfeild Ferrand, M.P., of St. Ives, Bingley, who at this time held the lordship of the manor of Haworth. I am obliged for this information from *The Manor of Haworth* by Kenneth Emsley (BST 20.35.1990).

Black Bull Hotel, c. 1856.

and the usual accompaniments of manufacturing industry, churches, schools, and tall mill chimneys. Around and on all sides are hills and deep dales, with long lines of stone fences crossing them in every direction. Viewed that morning, under the cheering influence of bright sunshine, the prospect was one of an agreeable description, for, although stone walls and mill chimneys are not exactly the thing in a picturesque point of view, yet they denote vigour in the capitalist, and ready money and employment to the teeming population. There cannot be a more gladdening sight than to look upon a district like this, where man has triumphed over the natural sterility of the soil and created happy homes for thousands who otherwise could not there have found the means of subsistence.

Descending an exceedingly steep road, we reach the foot of Haworth Street, and, after a heavy tug up its acute slope, are glad to find shelter in the Black Bull, a hostel rendered memorable by the story of the Haworth riots. A walk through the high-lying district we have endeavoured to describe is provocative of appetite, and nowhere can the wants of nature be better appeased than at the Black Bull.

Sallying out, we of course gazed at the church and the parsonage. The sight of the churchyard and the low wall adjoining the Black Bull brought vividly to our minds the story of the persecution of Mr Redhead and we could readily picture to ourselves the flight of the poor clergyman and his friends from their sooty assailants. An old man whom we met in the churchyard said that he was a singer in the church at the time when this strange affair occurred, and he told us that the sweep who was made the instrument to desecrate the house of God lamented the atrocious deed to his last hour, and spoke his sorrow for the act just before breathing his last. A writer in the *Daily News* doubts the truth as related by Mrs Gaskell, but the evidence of the old man, who resided there at the time, would appear to corroborate the main incidents.*

The church is in good repair, but it is plain and unostentatious in appearance. Mr Brontë's family repose in the interior. The schools, new and capacious, stand close by, and a little further on, grim, solitary, neglected and wretched looking, is the parsonage-house, a stone structure, ample in its proportions, but in no wise superior to the better class of farmhouses in the locality. It is surrounded by a high wall, topped with a thorn hedge, a wicket gate leading into the churchyard. At the side of the house rises the churchyard, so full of tombs that an additional piece of land has lately been added. With a melancholy pleasure we lingered about the spot, and thought over the lifelong struggles of the poor devoted creatures who had here spent their best days, neglected and unknown, Charlotte, however, always coming upwards as the bright star who led onwards to fame, but alas! that

* The reference to 'sooty assailants' clearly stems from Mrs Gaskell's account of the affair for which, however, there is little reliable evidence, although here we have apparent support for it. There is little doubt that Mr Redhead's determination to implement his appointment to the living at Haworth met with some unpardonable behaviour in the church from his opponents, but we may share with the writer in the *Daily News* his doubts about Mrs Gaskell's version of the affair which had, after all, occurred nearly forty years before.

Haworth Church in the time of the Brontës

fame came too late. Then, as we looked at that weatherbeaten house, and thought of the stern old man, left childless and alone, we could not help feeling for his troubles, although they had in a great measure been brought about by his own discipline and mode of life.* As we were leaving the churchyard, the Rev. Mr Nicholls, Charlotte's widower, passed in. He was in deep mourning, and truly did he seem 'a man of sorrow and acquainted with grief.'

There have been great changes in the district during the last twenty years, and Haworth has shared in the general prosperity, but the awkwardness of its position must deter any very great increase of population. Descend we now, well satisfied with our visit, and, passing through the 'turnpike', which guards the entrance to Haworth Street, we cross the 'brawling beck', ascend the steep bank, and are soon careering over the moors, en route for Bingley.

In conclusion we may say that, after having seen a good deal of the peasantry in various parts of the three kingdoms, nowhere have we experienced more kindness or civility than from the so-called rough

* A point of view not met with elsewhere.

population of the district among whom we spent a day. Rude are they in manners, and uncouth in speech, but there is an honesty and cuteness about them which cannot fail to be noticed...

A noticeable feature, too, we must not omit to record. Wherever any number of cottages were congregated, there stood a school, silently reminding us that some of the leading men of the district* were in the 'right place' and that they understand how to regenerate and render more polished the rough people around them.

The above excursion may seem a long walk to those who are not in the habit of pedestrianizing [!], but, taken in due season, and with suitable rest and refreshment at Haworth, any one gifted with moderate strength may undertake the journey. An easier route, and one which affords magnificent views, is by rail to Bingley, and thence over the moors to Haworth, returning by Keighley. The journey should not be undertaken unless on a fine clear morning, else it will be comparatively uninteresting. Those who are tempted to wander in these wild districts will find that the air is very provocative of health, rapid digestion, and sound sleep, three requisites of which many of our pent-up townsmen stand much in need.

* Patrick Brontë was most certainly one of them.

7

A Day at Haworth: A Reminiscence by the Rev. Thomas Akroyd, 1857

Brontë Society *Transactions* 19.49 (1986)
Contributed by Mr H. C. Harden

In the spring of 1857 the Rev. Thomas Akroyd, a Wesleyan minister, had an involuntary holiday: following a severe attack of bronchitis he was ordered away from South Liverpool, where he was then stationed, to the air of his native hills a little to the north of Halifax. He then rallied but was persuaded not to resume his duties too soon. Thereupon, accompanied by his two sisters and a fellow minister, he proceeded to spend a day visiting Haworth. His account of the visit was first published in *The City Road Magazine* in 1872:

> ... We put up at the Black Bull; ordered dinner and then sallied forth for observation or adventure as it might happen ... We betook ourselves to the churchyard and first looked up its plain, old weather-beaten fane, so rich now in various tradition; then at the renowned parsonage on its upper side, with its cold, gray walls, and its little patch of garden which opened into that drear 'God's acre'; and finally in the graves around us in which the *very* 'rude forefathers of the hamlet'* slept. As we were trying to decipher the inscription on a stone in the steeple of the church, we were challenged by one of the townsfolk meditating among the tombs. 'Now, con yo read that?' We replied that we could succeed tolerably up to a certain point. 'Ay', said he, 'monny folks can get as far as that, an' nobody can get much farther' ... We were subsequently guided by him to the parish clerk, who not only showed us into the church, but also proved to be a mine of useful and entertaining knowledge touching the Brontë family, and was happily as communicative as he was richly storied. He first led us to the east end of the church, where within the

* From *Elegy written in a country churchyard* by Thomas Gray.

communion railing lay the mother, brother and four sisters (Anne was buried at Scarborough). A plain mural tablet to the right of the communion-table was blackened with the sorrowful record of their births and deaths. Then he took us to the family pew, and said, with eyes brimming with tears, – how rare a thing in a sexton! – *She* sat i' this corner awlis', pointing to it as he spake; and by 'she'we found he meant Charlotte, who was evidently his special pride and favourite. Then, as we loitered about the church, he poured out a stream of most delightful gossip about them all in general and of *her* in particular. Amongst other things he told us how she had once sent him over to Leeds, to borrow from the office of the Baines'* a certain year's file of their *Mercury*; how he had the greatest difficulty in persuading those gentlemen to part with it, they naturally wondering much whatever Miss Brontë could want it for; how they at last consented to give it up to him on the express stipulation that it should be returned to them that very day fortnight; and how, as he walked home under his burden, he was as much puzzled as they to divine for what possible reason his mistress could have sent for it. 'But', this story ended with 'when *Shirley* coom out I saw it all then'; and *we* remembered how vividly one of the Luddite riots is described in that story. We spoke to him of Mrs Gaskell and her *Life*. He seemed a little injured that she had not sought his help for it; and surely it was a thing to be regretted, for her own sake if not for his. Wishing to test the authenticity, I said 'I suppose we must not believe everything in the book; such things, for instance, as Mr Brontë's being in the habit of firing off his superfluous excitement by a gun from the kitchen door.' 'I've 'eeard it hundreds of times' was his matter-of-fact reply. I asked if he thought Mr Brontë would see me if I called. He couldn't tell – Mr Brontë wur gettin' old and rather infirm now – didn't see monny folks; but he wur far readier than Mr Nicholls (the husband of Charlotte) – happen he might at such a time', etc., etc.

After dinner my desire to see Mr Brontë became irrepressible. So, going up to the house and putting my best manner to Martha, who answered the door, I begged her to take my card to her master, and ask if he would see me for a few minutes. She immediately returned radiant with smiles, and with the request that I would walk in. I followed her through the stone-floored passage to the room on one side of it which Mr Brontë occupied.

* Edward Baines was the editor of the *Leeds Mercury*.

He was a tall, thin man, of rather florid complexion, with weak eyes, over which he wore a green shade. His dress was of the orthodox black throughout, and his chin nestled in the capacious folds of an over-affluent neckcloth. He rose to greet me in the most courteous and affable manner, and then something like the following conversation followed:–

Mr B. – So you are from Liverpool, I see
T.A. – I am, Mr Brontë.
Mr B. – You have a church there, I suppose?
T.A. – No, I am a Wesleyan minister.
Mr B. – A what? (putting his hand behind his ear, for he was rather deaf).
T.A. – A Wesleyan minister.
Mr B. – O, indeed? A Wesleyan? Well, I have a great respect for the Wesleyans. I have known several of the ministers of your denomination. Very good men they were, very good men; and names are nothing to me – I care nothing about names. If we are only fighting under the banners of Jehovah – Jesus – that's the great thing. And the work of God is prospering amongst you in Liverpool, I hope?
T.A. – Yes, Mr Brontë. I am happy to say we are not labouring altogether in vain. We have large congregations and some fruit of our work amongst them.
Mr B. – I am very glad to hear it, I rejoice to hear it. I am not able to preach much myself now, but I am thankful to God I can still do a little. I generally preach once every Sunday and I am grateful for this.
T.A. – I hope you will excuse my intrusion upon you, but I have had a very great wish to see you and the neighbourhood which your gifted daughters have made so famous.
Mr B. – Yes I am very glad to see you. Of course, I cannot see all that come, you know. We have a great number of visitors now, and I am not able to see them all, but I am glad to see some of them – I am glad to see you.
T.A. – I have just read Mrs Gaskell's *Life of Charlotte Brontë* and have been intensely interested in it: but I suppose we must not take everything for gospel that Mrs G. has said about your family? (I remembered the reference to some of his own eccentricities, and conceived that he might not particularly like them).
Mr B. – Well, no. Mrs Gaskell is a novelist, you know, and we must allow her a little romance, eh? It is quite in her line. But the book is

substantially true, sir, for all that. There are some queer things in it, to be sure – there are some about myself, for instance – but the book is substantially true, sir, substantially true.

After a little more in the same strain I felt that I had sufficiently taxed his kindness and rose to take my leave. So he came with me to the door of the room, and shaking me very heartily by the hand bade me god-speed in my ministerial work and hoped that I might have many seals to my ministry, and win many souls for Jehovah-Jesus. 'So', as Bunyan says, 'I saw him no more'; but the memory of that old man's blessing is now one of the treasured things in my heart's reliquary.

He had rung the bell, so outside the room stood Martha to escort me to the door. But another wish clamoured to be gratified. So in the most seductive

The Duke of Wellington. The inscription reads: 'His Grace The Duke of Wellington, Field Marshal, etc., etc. Engraved from a daguerrotype portrait for which His Grace sat on May 1 1844'

tone I could summon I said: 'Martha, could I not see the portrait of Miss Brontë?' I don't know, sir', she replied. 'It is in Mr Nicholls' room and he doesn't like folks going in. But he isn't in it just now, he is in the back room. I'll go and ask him.' The clerk had previously told me of Mr N's reluctance to admit visitors into the parsonage; how, *e.g.*, he had recently declined the request of the daughters of Lord John Russell to see the picture, churlishly remarking that 'the house was not a picture gallery'. But – well done, Martha! here she comes with a gracious permission! So across the passage I stepped into whose *interior* had known so much of genius and so much of sorrow; that room in which the sisters had so often walked up and down arm-in-arm in the firelight, now excogitating the plots of their stories, and now consulting as to what should be done with their brilliant but erring brother. And there it hung on the wall, the portrait of Charlotte, by Richmond, for which she sat when in London; full of genius, and a sweet sadness; on a larger scale of course than the engraving from it prefixed to the memoir and giving me a much more agreeable impression of her. On another wall was the same artist's* portrait of her favourite hero, the Duke of Wellington, which gave her so much pleasure. And above and around the fireplace rose the shelves on which, arranged in admirable order, were those books the advent of which from her publishers was one of her few joys, dear soul !

We drove home in the gloaming, alternately chatting about what we had seen and heard, and singing snatches of sacred song; and so ended my day at Haworth.

* Not so. See previous page. See also page 21.

8

Dr Edward Benson visits Mr Brontë, January 1858

Brontë Society *Transactions* 8. Pt XLIV.136 (1934)

Towards the end of January 1858 Mr Brontë had a visit from Dr Edward White Benson (later Archbishop of Canterbury) who at that time was staying with his Sidgwick cousins, former pupils of Charlotte who was employed as their governess from May to July 1839.

In a letter to an old friend, J. B. Lightfoot, written from Riddlesden* on 25 January 1858, Dr Benson says: 'We are just going to ride over to Haworth – Charlotte Brontë's you know – and to see the place where high pressure misery wrought so much on genius.' Many years later the following letter from E. F. Benson, son of the Archbishop, appeared in *The Times* on 20 September 1933:

To the Editor of *The Times*

The following extract from a book of jottings by my father, dated January 25 1858, may be of interest to some of your readers:–

Rode over to Haworth. To-day it was a dismal place indeed to see, with a cold east wind blowing and a chill thick damp still obstinately clinging about all... Mrs Gaskell was very hasty and inaccurate in the steps she took to gain information, and never consulted Mr Nicholls or old Mr Brontë, as the latter himself told me. They never saw the book (*Life of Charlotte Brontë*) till it was in print. He lamented much the 'many unfounded things pertaining to our neighbours' which was therein related, and though he said there were also 'many ridiculous anecdotes about himself which never had existed except in some curious imaginations' this did not seem to move him. He

* See page 86.

seemed too old (80) and too composed to mind it... Mr Brontë thought the 3rd edition more truthful, but he said 'vulgar readers would prefer the 1st.'

He was in neat black, in a tiny room, with white thin locks and a powdered head, a Bible on the table the only visible book. He had preached the day before. His eye was keen. His talk was not only vigorous but clever. He spoke with interest of University reforms and talked of the time when he was a volunteer at St. John's, Cambridge, under fear of Napoleon's invasion. Everyone here knows that he changed his name in honour of Lord Nelson when the latter was made Duke of Brontē but it is so long ago that no-one knows what his name was.

The Clerk volunteered his information: he thought it very unjust to call Mr Brontë an 'austere' man, or to describe his shooting out of his door to relieve his temper. He used to shoot sparrows with a pistol, he said.

I am etc.
E. F. Benson

E. F. Benson was the author of a rather unsympathetic biography *Charlotte Brontë*, published by Longmans, Green & Co in 1932.

Here we have the third reference so far in these pages to Mr Brontë's habit of shooting daily from the parsonage. Ellen Nussey records precisely that the loading took place nightly with the discharge on the following morning from Mr Brontë's window. But who ever heard of someone trying to shoot sparrows with a pistol? Mr Brontë's action was probably a throwback to the time he and his family were living at Hartshead in the heart of the Luddite uprisings, where many God-fearing citizens nevertheless thought it prudent to have handy some effective means of defence. It is possible that Benson's informant had in mind the passage in *King Henry IV Pt. I* where Henry, Prince of Wales, describes the Earl of Douglas as 'he that rides at high speed, and with his pistol kills a sparrow flying.' (II.iv.341); but it is more likely that the morning discharge was a safety measure – the presence of a loaded weapon in the house in daytime would have been dangerous. In any event, the powder would have become damp.*

* See also pp. 67 and 107.

9

Walter White, an Early Visitor to Haworth, 1858

Brontë Society *Transactions* 16. Pt 3. 219 (1973)
Contributed by Mr J. Copley

In 1858 *A Month in Yorkshire* by Walter White was published by Chapman & Hall. A chapter in this book was devoted to a visit made by White to Haworth and Saltaire. He walked to Haworth from Keighley before breakfast:

> The factory people were going to work next morning – the youngsters clattering over the pavement in their wooden clogs – as I left the town by the Halifax road for Haworth, a walk of four miles, and all the way up-hill. The road runs along one side of a valley, which when the houses are left behind, looks pretty with numerous trees and fields of grass and wheat, and a winding brook, and makes a pleasing foreground to the view of the town. The road itself is neither town nor country; the foot-paths, as is not uncommon in Yorkshire, are paved nearly all the way, and houses are frequent, tenanted by weavers, with here and there a little shop displaying oaten bread. An hour of ascent and you come to cross-roads, where, turning to the right for about a furlong, you see Haworth, piled from base to summit of a steep hill, the highest point crowned by the church. The road makes a long bend in approaching the acclivity, which, if you choose, may be avoided by a cut-off; but coming as a pilgrim you will perhaps at first desire to see all. You pass a board which notifies *Haworth Town*, and then begins the ascent painfully steep, bounded on one side by houses; on the other – where you look into the valley – by little gardens and by a line of ragged little sheds and hutches. What a wearisome hill; you will half doubt whether horses can draw a load up it. Presently we have houses on both sides, and shops with plate-glass and mahogany mouldings,

contrasting strongly with the general rustic aspect, and the primitive shop of the Clogger.*

Some of the windows denote an expectation of visitors; the apothecary exhibits photographs of the church, the parsonage, and Mr Brontë; and no one seems surprised at your arrival. The Black Bull stands invitingly on the hill-top. I was ready for breakfast and the hostess quite ready to serve; and while I ate she talked of the family who made Haworth famous. She knew them all, brother and sisters; Mr Nicholls had preached the day before in the morning; Mr Brontë in the afternoon. It was mostly in the afternoon that the old gentleman preached, and he delivered his sermons without a book. The people felt sorry for his bereavements and they all liked Mr Nicholls.

The hostess had had a good many visitors, but expected 'a vast' before the summer was over.

The church is ugly enough to have had a Puritan for architect; and there, just beyond the crowded graves, stands the parsonage, as unsmiling as the church. After I had looked at it from a distance, and around on the landscape, which, in summer dress, is not dreary, though bounded by dark moors, the sexton came and admitted me to the church. He points to the low roof, and quotes Milton, and leads you to the family pew, and shows you the corner where *she*, that is, Charlotte – used to sit; and against the wall, but a few feet from this corner, you see the long plain memorial stone, with the melancholy list of names. As they descend, the inscriptions crowd close together; and beneath the lowest, that which records the decease of her who wrote *Jane Eyre*, there remains but a narrow blank for those which are to follow.

Then the sexton, turning away from the vestry, showed me in the marriage register the signatures of Charlotte Brontë, her husband and father; and next, his collection of photographs, with an intimation that they were for sale. When he saw that I had not the slightest inclination to become a purchaser, to have seen the place was quite enough; he said, that if I had a card to send in the old gentleman would see me. It seemed to me, I replied, that the greatest kindness a stranger could show the venerable pastor, would be, not to intrude upon him.

The sexton invited me to ascend the tower, but discovered that the key was missing; so, as I could not delay, I made a brief excursion on the moor behind the house, where heather-bloom masked the sombre hue; and then walked back to Keighley.

* A maker of clogs, or wooden soles for shoes.

10

A Ramble to Haworth in the Fifties by William Scruton

Bradford Weekly Telegraph, 23 April 1909

William Scruton's book about the Brontës, published in 1898, has already been referred to. Eleven years later he compiled the following article about a ramble he made to Haworth in 1858:

> ... It is almost needless to say that a pilgrimage to Haworth half a century ago was a very different matter to what it is to-day. The mode adopted by present-day visitors is, of course, to go by rail. Fifty years ago this was out of the question; unless one took the train to Keighley and did the remainder of the journey on foot through much tedious and uninteresting country. To those who did not mind a stretch of ten miles or so a much more pleasing route was that by way of Heaton, Wilsden, Old Allan and Brae Moor.
>
> This was the route taken by the writer of this sketch and a friend of literary and antiquarian tastes on a beautiful Sunday in the autumn of 1858. It proved to be the most delightful ramble through open, breezy country, with here and there some quaint old homesteads, and scenes of local historic interest.
>
> Leaving Cullingworth to the right, and on the left a small hamlet of cottages formerly inhabited by hand woolcombers, until we reached Brae, or Brow Moor Farm, from whence we had a fine view of Haworth right across the Worth Valley.
>
> It is an impressive sight to look upon the moorland village from this point of view, and one not soon to be forgotten. Its charm, however, is unknown to those who prefer to visit Haworth by rail.
>
> There is a bird's-eye view of the world-famed village, with its long stretch of moors beyond:–

'A distant, dreamy, dim blue chain
Of mountains circling every side.'

In the foreground of this rich world of solitude were distinctly visible the primitive church with grave-yard stretching around, and the quiet little parsonage in which had lived but a few years ago Charlotte Brontë, whose genius, after a sore struggle, had lifted her up out of obscurity into what Mrs Gaskell beautifully calls 'the everlasting hills of fame.' There, too, she died – when she had struggled through the wintry spring of her life, and its summer was just beginning to glow around her, – and there, in the bosom of the silent hills which nursed her genius, she slept.

After crossing the valley, Haworth was soon reached. Our previous conceptions of the village had been formed entirely from reading Mrs Gaskell's *Life of Charlotte Brontë* (issued the previous year – 1857), and we found all our expectations most gloriously disappointed.

We had supposed Haworth to be a scattered and straggling hamlet, with a desolate vicarage and a dilapidated church, surrounded and shut out from the world by a wilderness of barren heath.

Instead of that we found it transformed into a large and flourishing village – not a very enlightened or poetical place certainly, but quaint, compact and progressive, wherein we observed three large dissenting chapels and two or three good-sized schools.

Well, here we sat for a while in the churchyard, and close in front of us was the old parsonage house -now occupied by the father and husband of Charlotte Brontë – the residence of one of the most gifted families in all Britain. There the strange old-fashioned children had sat over the fire at night rehearsing mimic plays, and inventing wondrous stories of fabulous adventure There the three girls, shut out from the world, produced works of fiction that will live as long as the language in which they are written. There they thought, hoped, planned, and suffered; there they struggled, unassisted, with their destiny, and triumphed. There, one by one, they died, in the morning of their days and the culminating glory of their genius. Verily, in that house was acted a tragedy most mournful, yet most sublime...

At the inn where we put up we had the good fortune to meet with a young maidservant who had sometimes been called into the parsonage to wait upon Mr Brontë during the temporary absence of the regular domestic. In an unsophisticated Yorkshire fashion she gave us some interesting particulars of the Brontë family. She had seen Miss Brontë when writing her books, and had often carried large parcels for her to the post, and wondered what was in them. She was very small, and Emily was bigger a good deal. They were all great walkers, and used to go on to the moors for hours together. She had seen Mrs Gaskell, but didn't know about her. After Miss Brontë's marriage she never got the better of a cold she caught going one winter's day on to the moor to the waterfall, which Mrs Gaskell called a 'cascade'.

As we wished to see the interior of the church before the afternoon service commenced we had to cut short the girl's reminiscences, and after thanking her for all she had told us we made our way to the ancient fabric upon which, as yet, the hand of the despoiler had not been laid.

Inside the church we were shown the new monumental slab containing the names of the Brontës who slept below the communion table, except the one (Anne), who had died and was interred at Scarborough. Sufficient space was left on the slab for the entry of another name which ere long would be added to the list. What thoughts rushed to one's mind while standing by the hallowed dust of the talented women who had been so early swept away by the fell-destroyer – death !

The interior of the old church has been so often described by various writers that it is needless to dwell upon the subject here. Having seen the chief objects of interest, good Sunday though it was, we retired until the congregation came and took their places in the old high-backed oak pews, on which were conspicuously painted the names of their respective owners.

To pass the interval we spent the time in reading the inscriptions on the tombstones, still intending to enter the church in time for the service – a great inducement to do so being the possibility of hearing Mr Brontë preach as he only did in the afternoon, when his health would permit. We now took our seats in the church, and after a while a tall, venerable looking old man, with hair as white as snow and a face full of intelligence and benevolence, entered the sacred edifice, walked down the aisle and mounted the three-decker pulpit to preach what was then known as 'the afternoon sermon.' This was the Rev. Patrick Brontë. His appearance, to say the least, could not fail to inspire feelings of profound reverence. He had a fine intelligent face indicative of a power and energy which are merely mellowed by time and shaded somewhat mournfully by sufferings. One glance at that physiognomy sufficed to show that its possessor had been shaped by nature after a model of its own – a man of strong passions, but stronger self-control; of warm affections, but adamantine will – a man possibly eccentric, but whose eccentricities merely proved the positive tendency of his being and the strength and struggles of his soul.

It was sad to see this venerable man, and to know that of all his children – the gifted, the admired, the affectionate – not one was left.

The sermon was preached extemporary in a quiet, homely, conversational style and without any attempt at declamation. His only object seemed to be to explain fully all the circumstances connected with the subject of his text, and having done so, concluded without any formal application, and left his congregation to apply it for themselves.

The service ended, Mr Brontë quietly left the church, accompanied by his son-in-law, the Rev. A.B. Nicholls, who had occupied the reading desk.

After the congregation had departed we loitered for a while in the now silent sanctuary. It seemed as if the very presence of the revered patriarch had filled the place with an atmosphere of sanctity not easy to describe.

On our return journey later in the day we took a parting look at the village from the opposing hill – a last glance at the old parsonage, the square towered church, and the long, straggling street below, all reposing peacefully in the light of declining day. The mellow gleam of an autumn sunset flushed the western sky, and was shaded calmly off into a cloudless twilight. The stars glimmered through the pale blue heavens, and the solemn hush of evening rested like a benediction on mill and homestead, on brook and mountain.

So ended our first ramble to Brontë-land, the home of that talented sisterhood who had made this moorland village memorable for all time. It was by no means our last visit, but as with the author who never forgets his first appearance in print, or the orator his first speech, so we can never erase from memory the impressions left upon it by this our first pilgrimage to Haworth.

William Scruton was of course writing with hindsight and after his occasional purple patches we come now to the calm and measured account of an academic from Dublin which played its part years later in solving what had been a longstanding mystery about one of the family groups painted by Branwell.

11

John Elliot Cairnes' Visit to Haworth Parsonage, September 1858

Brontë Society *Transactions* 18. Pt 4.292 (1984)

It was in 1984 that Dr Timothy Foley of the Department of English at University College, Galway, sent to Haworth the following extract from a long letter which John Elliot Cairnes, Professor of Political Economy at Trinity College, Dublin, wrote to a friend on his return from a meeting in Leeds in 1858 of the British Association for the Advancement of Science. Professor Cairnes was apparently not impressed with Leeds and for him a visit to Haworth provided a memorable diversion:

> . . . The visit I enjoyed most was one which I made by myself. It was to the village of the scene of Charlotte Brontë's life. The village is exactly as described by Mrs Gaskell, consisting of a single street on the side of a very steep hill, with the church and parsonage at the top. On going up the street I passed a small grocer's shop, which seemed to serve also as a book shop for the village, for in the window, amongst a few other books, were copies of *Villette*, *Shirley* and *Jane Eyre* in great abundance. I went in, bought a copy of *Villette* and began to talk to the old woman behind the counter about the Brontës. She was a very nice old dame (not very old either; indeed she told me afterwards she was only older by six months than Charlotte Brontë would have been had she been alive; but she looked much more than this) and entered very freely into conversation on the subject I had in view. It was from her that the Brontë girls used to obtain their paper, when the Keighley supply was exhausted, and she mentioned the way in which the increasing demand at the parsonage led her to increase her stock while she was puzzled to guess the purpose for which all the foolscap was wanted. Branwell Brontë seemed to be a special favourite of hers,

and, as she spoke of his good heartedness, and then of his lapses, the tears came into her eyes.

From this good dame I learned where the sexton lived, whom, having found, I proceeded with to the Church. There I saw the tablet, described by Mrs Gaskell, the stone under which lay poor Charlotte, the parsonage pew on one side of which, 'with their backs to the congregation 'used to sit Emily and Anne, (because, as the sexton explained) 'they were always the strangest'; while the cross bench half facing the congregation was the seat of Charlotte. I learned from the sexton that Mr Brontë still preaches every Sunday afternoon, unless suffering from attacks of illness – unfortunately I did not know this in time; had I done so I should certainly have gone to hear him. It occurred to me that it might not be amiss if I paid my respects to the old gentleman; – and, on being told by the sexton, in answer to my inquiry, that this had been done by some others who had been well received, I sent in my card. I was informed that Mr Brontë had, a few hours previously, retired to bed, not feeling well, but that he hoped I would walk in and see the house. This I, of course, did under the guidance of the maid, Martha (mentioned by Mrs Gaskell). She is an interesting looking girl with very dark eyes and hair, and would be pretty but for the loss of nearly all her front teeth. She shewed me first the parlour with Charlotte's portrait on the dark side of the room, fronting a medallion cast of Branwell on the other, while on either side of the door, there was the Duke of Wellington and Thackeray. There was also her little library, not above sixty or seventy volumes in all, but a most choice collection . . . Amongst others I noticed the *Life of Sterling*, *Sartor Resartus*, Newman on the Soul,* and books of that cast, her fondness for which showed what a great revolution her religious views had undergone from that early time, when she used to correspond with Ellen Nussey in the sickly pietistic strain – a revolution, by the way, of the progress of which it would have been most interesting to have had some record, but which Mrs Gaskell scarcely seemed to be aware of, leaving her readers to discover it only by its results.

On the walls of the opposite room – the old gentleman's study – were some period drawings of Charlotte, and a water painting by Emily of 'Keeper', with a cat and a small dog. By the by I asked Martha about the story of Emily's chastisement of Keeper by pounding him with her

* *The Soul; her Sorrows and her Aspirations* (1849) by Francis Newman, brother of Cardinal Newman. 'Have you read this work? It is daring, – it may be mistaken, – but it is pure and elevated.' Charlotte Brontë to James Taylor in a letter dated 1 October 1849. (SHB III 26–27).

fists; but she declared she could remember nothing of it, although she said she must have been in the family at the time the incident occurred – She said, however, she had more than once seen Emily separate Keeper from other dogs when fighting, and testified to her courage in that respect. I suspect Mrs Gaskell does not scrutinize over-carefully the authority of her stories, if they be only picturesque. The oil-painting Mrs Gaskell speaks of by Branwell* of the three sisters is on the first landing on the way upstairs – It is a shocking daub, not up to the rudest sign board style. The artist stands himself in the middle with bright red hair divided down the centre, and a straight line along the nose to mark its highest point.

Mrs Gaskell speaks of Branwell as handsome, but from what I could learn of the villagers this was not the case. The innkeeper at Keighley, from whom I hired my cab, speaking to me of him, said, 'he was as well as the sisters any how.' I had been disappointed at being told by every one to whom I talked on the subject (except Martha) that the girls were *so* plain. When I asked the old woman in the bookshop which of them was the best looking, she shook her head and said there was not much to choose amongst them in that respect – The sexton thought Anne the best looking, but indeed he could not say much for her looks. Yet the portrait in the parlour [by George Richmond] of which that prefixed to Mrs Gaskell's work is a facsimile (and of which I bought from the sexton a photograph) -this portrait is to my taste anything but that of an ordinary woman (in either sense of that word); and Martha avers that it does not flatter – *that it is very like*. On the whole I shall believe Martha, and continue to think of Charlotte as I see her in my photograph. But perhaps the most interesting part of the proceedings was the perusal of Charlotte Brontë's letters, a small bundle of which, on my asking Martha if she had any, was produced. Some of them appear in the biography; there were others which are not there. They were all addressed to Martha; generally commencing with some directions concerning household matters, and concluding with a brief description of where she was, what she was doing, and so forth. They were in the gentlest and kindest vein, with an occasional dash of humour, but never passing beyond that which was perfectly natural in a mistress addressing her favourite maid. Unfortunately, as I devoured the letters, the day wore on, and the train was approaching, and I was obliged to leave off, my meal half

* That was the Pillar portrait. What Cairnes describes here is the Gun Group.

An unknown artist's impression of Branwell Brontë's 'Gun Group' which appeared in J. Horsfall Turner's *Haworth Past and Present* published in 1879.

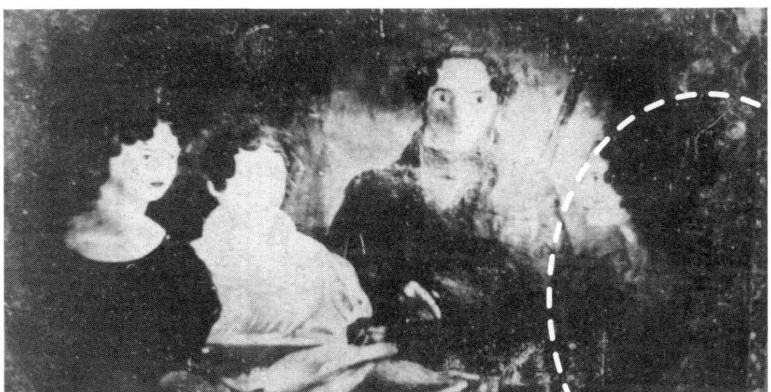

The photograph below left was discovered in 1989 and is of the painting which Professor Cairnes mistakenly thought was that described by Mrs Gaskell. It is in fact the 'Gun Group' destroyed by Mr Nicholls with the exception of the fragment of Emily (below) which is in the National Portrait Gallery.

'The artist stands himself in the middle with bright red hair'.

John Elliot Cairnes, September 1858
(see page 50)

'The artist himself figured in the picture. He was represented in the middle of the canvas with a gun resting on the ground, dividing the picture by an awkward line.'

William Davis, Autumn 1858
(see page 56)

untouched. I departed most reluctantly, oft looking back on the old Church and parsonage, and the steep straggling village, and finally took my way hence, pondering deeply on the strange sad story of which I had been tracing the memorials.

I have gone into these matters at this length, partly because I thought they might interest you, and partly because I wish to impress on my own memory the incidents of the visit; for I can scarcely express the admiration and respect which I feel for the genius and character of Charlotte Brontë, and am unwilling to part with any impressions that may give vividness to my conception of her.

So ended the fascinating letter unearthed by Dr. Foley.

Cairnes was familiar with Mrs Gaskell's *Life* but was wrong in thinking that the painting he saw was that described by her as 'divided, almost down the middle, by a great pillar.' The question then arises: could it have been the 'Gun Group'? Mr Nicholls told Mr Shorter in 1895 that after Mr Brontë's death he removed it [the Gun Group] to Ireland and being of the opinion that the only accurate portrait was that of Emily, he cut this out and destroyed the remainder. The Emily fragment was given to Martha Brown on one of her visits to Mr Nicholls but after her death it was returned to him and is now in the National Portrait Gallery along with the 'Pillar Portrait'.

The matter was finally resolved in 1989 when a very poor and faded photograph was discovered in New Orleans among the papers of the late Professor Mildred Christian, an eminent American Brontë researcher, which was clearly that of the original 'Gun Group' painting. It was subsequently established that the photograph had been intended for inclusion in J. Horsfall Turner's *Haworth Past and Present*, published in 1879, but because of its poor quality an unknown artist was commissioned to produce an impression of the painting to be used instead.* This artistic impression was all that we knew about the group until Cairnes' letter came to light, apart from a few tracings made from it before its destruction. According to the ages of the sisters written on the back of the tracings the group was painted in 1834.**

* See also pp. 56 and 113.

** According to Dr Juliet Barker the Gun Group was possibly photographed by John Moore, the Haworth chemist. (BST 20.10.1990).

12

Haworth Thirty-seven Years Ago by William Davies, 1858

Temple Bar Magazine: a London Magazine for Town and Country Readers, January 1896

William Davies came to Haworth at about the same time as Professor Cairnes and also describes the Gun Group painting, but whereas Cairnes' reference to the painting was contained in a letter which, as far as is known, remained unpublished until it appeared in *Brontë Society Transactions* for 1984, the article by Davies appeared as early as 1896 in a magazine on sale to the public. At that time there was surely a possibility (which never materialised) that someone, already aware of the impression in Horsfall Turner's book and reading the account below, would have realised that Davies was describing the same painting. Such action would have been a step forward, but the complete solution to the Gun Group mystery had to wait until the discovery of that old photograph in New Orleans in 1989.

> ... It was in the autumn of 1858 that I made a visit to Haworth in Yorkshire in the company of a friend for the purpose of seeing the home of the Brontë sisters, whose works have made so notable a mark in the literary history of the century... Some record of this visit may not be uninteresting to those of a newer generation, as not only is the last lineal descendant of the Brontë family now passed away, but I believe the very neighbourhood has become so changed as to be scarcely recognisable.
>
> One Friday evening in September my friend and I arrived at the Keighley railway station in a drenching rain, which caused us to look out for night quarters in that town, and to delay the completion of our journey until the following morning. We started on foot next

morning, which was bright and cheery, for Haworth, to which there was no railway at that time – a walk of about four miles. Keighley, then a small country town, was extending its limits in a wider area. The road was mostly uphill, with a scattering of houses almost the whole distance...

The village of Haworth at that time consisted of a single street precipitously steep, surmounted by the church, the parsonage, and the Black Bull inn. The parsonage was a bare, stone, squarely-built house with a small garden in front, separated by a tall thorn fence from a well-filled graveyard, within the limits of which stood the stalwart old church; thence a pathway led over two or three fields on to broad, undulating moors, over which the sun seemed to shine with peculiar lustre, and the wind blew freshly, fragrant with the odour of heath and ling. Upland slopes were seen crowned with tiny towns, yet built firm and massive as bastions, each house of stone with its windows in groups, generally three together – one large central one and two smaller side ones. The open moorland was broken by hollows or dingles, through which streams, or becks as they are called, ran murmuringly, feeding

Parsonage, Sunday School and old Church, pre 1861.

Haworth Church and Parsonage. Drawn by Mrs Gaskell 1855.

many mills in their course. Of these features there seemed to be endless repetition, over which sunshine and shadow chased each other through all the changeful day.

At the Black Bull, so associated with Brontë annals, we took up our abode during our sojourn. Here we met the sexton, who took us into the church, showing us the Brontë pew and the memorial tablets of the family deceased. The parsonage was, like the rest of the houses in the neighbourhood, built of sandstone, square, harsh in line and, it must be confessed, ugly; not at all like the picturesque tenement vignetted by Mrs Gaskell's book, by which a quite incorrect idea of its outline and proportion, as well of the configuration of the church, is given. The sexton asked us if we had a wish to see Mr Brontë. Of course we said we had a desire to do so, but at the same time expressed a diffidence in intruding upon him as strangers. He told us, however, that occasionally Mr Brontë was pleased to receive visitors, even though strangers, on his days of better health, and said if we would send our names he would ask him. This we did, and an invitation was sent to us to call in the afternoon.

We were introduced into a room to the left of the entrance known as Mr Nicholls' room. Upon the walls were hung Mr Richmond's pastel drawing of Charlotte Brontë, so well known by the engraving; there were also engraved portraits of Wellington and Thackeray, and a medallion portrait in plaster of Branwell Brontë. We were taken to the room of Mr Brontë on the right. He met us as we entered. This room was his study, barely and simply furnished. From the account of Mr Brontë given by Mrs Gaskell and from biographical hints dropped by Charlotte, I had expected another kind of person with a different manner. At that time he was eighty-one, the melancholy survivor of a wife and six children, a tall and dignified gentleman of the old school, with easy manners and courteous bearing, and that stamp of breeding which often distinguishes the Englishman of high birth and ancestral surroundings.[!] We had an interesting talk with him upon the members of his family as well as on the topics of the day. We spoke of the great social and other changes he had seen in the course of his lifetime and questioned if we should live to witness so many. He replied that it was likely we might do so, 'for,' he said, 'there is none of us who knows what may lie in the womb of the future*'. The recently published biography of Charlotte Brontë was discussed. 'It is full of lies,' he said; 'but since it appears to amuse the public it is of no importance to me.' This was in allusion to the disparaging stories told of himself. On coming away we were shown a painting on the staircase of the sisters by their brother Branwell. It was crude and harsh from a technical point of view, but the likenesses were said to be good. The artist himself figured in the picture. He was represented standing in the middle of the canvas with a gun resting on the ground, dividing the picture by an awkward line. The details are not very clear to me at this length of time, but I remember thinking that the portrait of Emily bore a resemblance to the sweet face of the figure looking out of the picture of Millais' *Autumn Leaves*.

On leaving the house we were taken across the moors to visit a waterfall which was a favourite haunt of the sisters. One could easily understand the inspiration of such scenery; the swelling and sweeping moorlands, the fresh wind, the changing sky, the hollows and ravines, which often concealed a mill, and the stream utilised in manufacture. We then went on to an old manorial farm called 'Heaton's of Ponden', which we were told was the original model of Wuthering

* *Othello* I.iii.75.

Heights, which indeed corresponded in some measure to the description given in Emily Brontë's romance. An inscription carved in stone over the front door stated that the house had been first built by Robert Heaton for his son Michael in the year 1634, that additions had been made by his grandson, Robert Heaton, in A.D. 1680, and that there had been some rebuilding by his descendant R.H. in 1801. The mullioned windows and stout walls brought vividly to mind the representations of the story. The pines described as slanting at the gable appeared, however, to be borrowed from an eminence between Stanbury and Haworth, on which there was a house with three pines blown slantwise by the wind. The scenery and surroundings of the whole neighbourhood seemed to me to be so much in consonance with the descriptions of scenery given in the various books of the sisters that I fancied I should have been able to have detected the locality of their authorship if I had not been otherwise aware of it. Indeed, I noticed the name Earnshaw somewhere in the neighbourhood of Haworth, which at once recalled to me the proprietorship of Wuthering Heights. One would hardly have been surprised to have seen the stalwart figure of Hareton slouching out of this old house, or the more decorous form of Heathcliff leaning by the doorway; but nothing of the sort met our view. A few words with the indwellers, who were plain farming folks, and we returned to our inn.

Charlotte appeared to have been the favourite in the neighbourhood. About Emily there seemed to be little known. She was a negative or neutral in popular regard, which is what one would expect of one whose intellectual power and gifts lay so far from the everyday lines and ordinary phases of life. She evidently enjoyed the respect of all, but did not call forth a more positive sentiment, simply because she was not known out of the reserves of her very undemonstrative nature.

In the evening we met some of the boon companions of Branwell Brontë at the inn, who entertained us with many anecdotes of his intellectual ability and humorous sharpness. I remember one of these anecdotes was that he was standing with a companion by a shop window in Keighley, in which there was displayed the picture of a man riding upon an ass. His friend remarked that the figure thus seated bore a resemblance to Branwell, upon which, without a word, Branwell jumped upon his back. Another story I remember was of a commercial traveller who was describing some part of London, when Branwell corrected him upon a mistaken locality. The circumstance was warmly contested, but finally a map of London was procured, and Branwell was found to be right. The remarkable fact about this was that though Branwell had never been to London, he had a knowledge of the complete geography of the city – even, I was told, to its smaller streets and lanes.

One of his cronies said that he often carried with him a huge volume – a sort of commonplace book – in which he would write with either hand and at the same time maintain an undistracted conversation. He once created great amusement by reading from this book a humorous account of a Methodist Prayer or Revival Meeting. Other stories were related of him, some, it must be confessed, not to his credit, yet he was apparently much appreciated, even beloved by the people of the place. Tears gathered to the eyes of the wife of a tradesman in the village as she narrated to us some of the worthier traits of his character.

The Rev. Patrick Brontë c. 1860. 'He wore an enormous cravat . . . his fingers were long and skinny, almost of the nature of talons . . .'

On the Sunday morning we went to church. Mr Nicholls officiated, a man of pleasing , and what the Italians would call a *simpatico* personality. One seemed to discern in him a harmonious and kindly nature, and the worthy husband of a good woman. There was a large congregation in the afternoon, Mr Nicholls officiating as before. During the reading of the first lesson, with the steps of age, solemn and slow, robed in black gown, Mr Brontë came in and seated himself in the old-fashioned square pew. At the final hymn he went into the pulpit and gave a vigorous and impressive discourse, no word of which was lost upon the listeners It might have been considered a model sermon in many respects. Yet there was a element of the grotesque in its delivery, though it was without the least affectation or mannerism of any sort. He wore an enormous white cravat, which covered the features up to the level of the ears. When he wished to be particularly impressive, he seemed to emerge from this receptacle and then gradually retire into it. His fingers were long and skinny, almost of the nature of talons, and were displayed on the pulpit cushion. This gave something of an eerie appearance to the preacher, and perhaps added to the impressiveness of his discourse, which in all respects was one to be remembered . . .

Branwell's knowledge of the geography of London streets could have been acquired in preparation for his planned visit to the Royal Academy Schools in 1835, but there has been for some time considerable doubt, in the absence of reliable evidence, as to whether the visit ever took place, a view strengthened by this 1858 account. The matter has surely been put beyond all doubt by an unpublished letter recently acquired by the Brontë Society. It is signed jointly by Mr Brontë and Branwell, dated 16 November 1835, and addressed to William Robinson, the Leeds portrait painter. Branwell states that his father has resolved upon his receiving a further course of lessons during the winter 'in addition to those you have already given me'; Mr Brontë expresses his pleasure at the progress his son has made and states his decision that 'he should improve himself further in anatomy . . . and also in the classics, and consequently defer his journey to London till next summer . . .'

13

Charlotte Brontë by the Rev. Canon Bardsley

Brontë Society *Transactions* 2.Pt IX.30 (1899)

The Rev. Canon Bardsley, Vicar of Huddersfield, addressed a meeting of the Brontë Society in January 1899 in which he recalled a visit to Haworth not long after Charlotte's death:

> ... In my early manhood I accompanied my father to Haworth. While my father was in the bedroom where Mr Brontë was seriously ill, and while Mr Nicholls was in the Parish, I went through the library of the gifted authoress; specially noted *Vanity Fair* and *Henry Esmond* with the inscriptions of their author; read some pencil notes written on the margin of books in Charlotte Brontë's well-known microscopic hand; and gazed upon her portrait by Richmond, and those of the Duke of Wellington and Thackeray – the one the hero of her early years and the other of her later days...
>
> I need not tell you how many of our cousins from across the ocean have made a pilgrimage to Haworth Parsonage as to a sacred shrine. They admire the works of Charlotte Brontë as much, and perhaps even more, than we. As we rejoice to-day in the closer alliance between England and the United States, and remember that few influences link nations together more firmly than a common literature, we will not forget that Charlotte Brontë has had her part in cementing this happy union.
>
> After dinner, Mr Nicholls took me on his wife's favourite walk on the moors. My companion was kindness itself, but not a spark of enthusiasm could I evoke. I thought at the time that Charlotte Brontë had been drawn to her husband as a hop pillow attracts itself to the weary head and restless brain, but I found afterwards that I had formed a

hasty and mistaken judgment. We are all indebted to Mr Clement Shorter for the noble tribute he has paid to the character of Mr Arthur Nicholls.*

As I returned with my father to Keighley, he told me how distressed he had been to see the tears in the eyes of old Mr Brontë while he spoke of the aspersions on his domestic character, and the exaggerated statements with reference to the eccentricities of his daily life, in Mrs Gaskell's memoir of his daughter, which had just been published. The author of Charlotte Brontë's *Life* was a kindred genius with her whose portrait she has drawn with all the charm of her literary skill. I have no need in this assembly to refer to the grave faults in the early editions of this work, which have disappeared from the later ones.

If I venture to hint that a certain exaggeration still remains, some devoted admirer of Mrs Gaskell in this audience may think of the aphorism – 'The defects of the great are the consolation of the dunces'...

* Canon Bardsley probably had in mind Clement Shorter's *Charlotte Brontë and Her Circle*, published by Hodder & Stoughton in 1896, which had a chapter devoted to Mr Nicholls. The two men had met in 1895 when Shorter went to Banagher, probably at the behest of T. J. Wise, and persuaded Nicholls to sell some of the Brontëana he had brought from Haworth in 1861.

14

An American Visitor for Mr Brontë by James M. Hoppin

Brontë Society *Transactions* 15.Pt 4.327 (1969)

At about the time of Canon Bardsley's visit there arrived at Haworth a professor from Yale, James M. Hoppin. He was in the course of a comprehensive tour of England, an account of which, *The Old Country: Its Scenery, Art and People*, was published by Sampson Low, Son and Marston, London, in 1867. He arrived at Keighley via Bolton Abbey and it is in Keighley that his account begins:

> Keighley has been chiefly made known to us from its proximity to Haworth, Charlotte Brontë's home. When did we ever hear or think about it before? Yet it is one of those important and swarming manufacturing places that make the power and wealth of England; and, as I arrived on pay-day afternoon, the streets were thronged with thousands of factory people bearing the hard and independent stamp of West Riding weavers, described so vigorously in *Shirley*. In the dull and up-hill ride of four miles to Haworth, shut in most of the way by high stone walls, instead of the usual green hedges, I could not but think of those two feeble sisters, struggling along afoot over this dreary road, in the thunderstorm, on their way to Keighley to take the London train, for the purpose of proving to their publisher their actual and separate identity. We passed several great stone walls that might have been very well used for fortresses.
>
> Haworth was pointed out with its gray tower, near the summit of a very high hill, and at its back swept away north the rolling, dismal moorlands, without the sign of human habitation. A month later, and these moors would be gorgeous with heather-blossoms.

After passing a few straggling houses, we began to ascend that long, steep, paved street of Haworth, now become so well known. What a straining pull of it! At the top was the Black Bull inn. Just at the left of the inn, within a step or so, through a tall iron gate, was the populous cemetery of the church.

The church itself is a plain, stone building, less interesting, architecturally, than English village churches usually are. The tower is evidently of very ancient date, with a modern body pinned upon it. All was hard, weather-worn stone, with nothing green or smiling; there was not a tuft of grass about the churchyard. I could not help glancing at the Parsonage, looking over the edge of the tabled graveyard; but I hastened into the church and was seated in the Squire's pew near the pulpit, hung with faded green baize.

Mr Nicholls preached from John v. 1. He is a dark-complexioned man, rather thin, with black hair and beard. It was a short, practical sermon, and the tones of his voice, especially in the service, were grave and pleasant, and, as I conceived, with a touch of sadness. The plaintive litany seemed never more appropriate. It was a gusty day of rain and shine, but its general complexion was melancholy.

The old pews within were so dull and brown, the old tombs outside were so still and sad, and the roar and dashing of the storm at times was so dismal, that the sins, conflicts, and sorrows of life would have been the sermon preached to one's heart had the preacher charmed never so sweetly. I saw the pew, and the corner of it, where Charlotte used to sit; and the new white marble tablet on the wall, erected to her memory, and that of her mother, four sisters and brother . . .

Without intending or seeking it, I was invited, as a stranger, to call upon Mr Brontë, for a few moments during the intermission. I went through a high-walled yard at the back of the house, around to the front, through a small flower-garden (rather run to waste now) and was shown by Martha into Mr Brontë's study.

I do not think it would be violating good taste to speak of an interview so simple, and that had nothing confidential in its character. Mr Brontë met me with real kindness of manner, but with something of the stateliness of the old school. His hair, worn short, was white as driven snow; his ample cambric cravat completely covered his chin; and his black dress was of the most scrupulous neatness. He has been called handsome, but that he never could have been. He has strong, rugged, even harsh features, with a high, wrinkled forehead, and swarthy complexion; and his eyes are partially closed, for he is almost blind.

He said he was induced to invite me to his house, though he saw very little company, because he learned I was an American, and he thought much of America.

Our conversation was chiefly upon religious topics, and he wished to be informed about the great spiritual movements which from time to time pass over America. He thought that revivals in England and Ireland were accompanied by too much animal excitement; yet he believed in their reality... He spoke of education in England – that was all the fashion just now; but I could not help thinking that the conservative, granite-minded old Helstone looked upon a great deal of it as sentimental and superficial. He struck me as being naturally a social man, with a mind fond of discussion, and feeding eagerly on new ideas, in spite of his reserve. My call was necessarily quite a short one.

I then went into the opposite parlour, where his daughters used to sit and write. There was Charlotte's portrait, with those large, dark eyes, square impending brow, and sad, unsmiling mouth. Branwell Brontë's medallion likeness hung opposite; and Thackeray's portrait, 'looking past her' as she said, was on the front wall. Her books still lay on the table. There was a Bible of Emily's*, and a much-worn copy of Mrs Gaskell's *Mary Barton,* presented by the authoress to Mrs Nicholls. This room had rather a pleasant look, but its furnishing was simple to severity, and its only ornament was a little bunch of broom-grass on the table. Martha then showed me into the kitchen for a moment. This had been Tabby's kingdom. Everything was exquisitely neat, and the copper pans shone like gold. It was a snug, warm, crooning** place; and it was not difficult to see the picture, on a dark winter eve, when the storms howled over the moor and rattled against the windows, of those bright-fancied children crouching together around the fire, telling their strange stories and living in a world created by themselves. Here Emily Brontë studied German, with her book propped up before her, while she kneaded dough. Now all are gone and the old father, shutting up many things in his own impenetrable mind, was living on alone, thinking more perhaps of meeting his children again in a sinless and sorrowless world, than of all their fame in this.

* Still in the Parsonage.

** Definitions of this word, as listed in *The English Dialect Dictionary* ed. by Joseph Wright 1898 include 'to make a low monotonous sound or murmur.'

In the afternoon I heard Mr Brontë preach from Job iii 17: 'There the wicked cease from troubling; and there the weary be at rest.' It was the simple extemporaneous talk of an aged pastor to his people, spoken without effort, in short, easy sentences, – and was drawn, it appeared to me, *right out of that old graveyard*, among whose stones his feet had walked, and his imagination had lived so long. In parts it was pathetic, especially where he alluded to the loss of children. He branched off upon the sorrows, convulsions, and troubles then in the world, and he seemed to long for wings like a dove to fly away from this changeful scene, and be at rest. The old church clock, as if echoing the venerable preacher's remarks, had written on it 'Time how short – eternity how long!'

On the whole, my Haworth visit was a serious and sobering one. I thought of what Charlotte Brontë said, that 'it always made her unhappy to go away from Haworth, for it took her so long to become happy after she got home.' Yet that stone house a century old, those bleak moors, that very melancholy crowded graveyard, may have done something to make Charlotte Brontë what she was. They fenced her in, and made her inventive. Her fiery Irish imagination was concentrated here into a vital energetic current, that did not waste itself in endless poetic mazy streams, but cut for itself a deep, practical, and creative channel...

15

An American Visitor: H. J. Raymond

Charlotte Brontë: A Monograph by T. Wemyss Reid (Macmillan & Co., London, 1877) pp. 193/196

Another American who came to Haworth after the death of Charlotte was Mr H. J. Raymond, for many years editor of *The New York Times*.

In an account he wrote later, quoted by Wemyss Reid, he recalled how, on his railway journey to Keighley, he 'astonished an intelligent, sociable, and very agreeable English lady, his sole companion in the railway carriage, by telling her the errand which had brought him to Yorkshire. She lived in the neighbourhood, had read the *Jane Eyre* novels, and supposed the girls were clever but she would not go ten steps to see where they lived, nor could she understand how a stranger from America should feel any interest in their affairs.'

Arrived at Haworth, and having satisfied himself as to the appearance of the parsonage and the character of the surrounding neighbourhood, Mr Raymond went to the Black Bull to dine and sleep:

> As I took my candle to go to my chamber, I stepped for a moment into the kitchen, where the landlord and landlady were having a comfortable chat over pipes and ale, with a companionable rustic of the place, who proved to be a nephew of the old servant Tabby, who lived so long, and at last died in the service of the Brontë family. I joined the circle, and sat there till long after midnight. Branwell was clearly the hero of the village worship. A little red-headed fellow, the landlord said, quick, bright, abounding in stories, in jokes, and in pleasant talk of every kind; he was a general favourite in the town, and the special wonder of the Black Bull circles.
>
> The next morning I prepared to call at the parsonage. I was told that Mr Brontë and Mr Nicholls declined to receive strangers, having a great aversion to visits of curiosity, and being exceedingly retiring and

reserved in their habits. I sent in my card, however, and was shown into the little library at the right of the entrance, where I was asked to await Mr Nicholls's appearance. The room was small, very plainly furnished, with small bookcases round the walls, the one between the windows containing copies of the Brontë novels. Mr Nicholls soon came in and made me welcome. To my apologies for my intrusion he assured me that while they were under the necessity of declining many visits, both he and his father [*sic*] were always happy to see their friends, and that the words 'New York' upon my card were quite sufficient to ensure me a welcome. Mr Brontë, he said, was not up when I called, but had desired him to detain me until he could dress and come down, as he did soon after. I had an exceedingly pleasant conversation of half an hour with them both ... Mr Brontë's personal appearance is striking and peculiar. He is tall, thin, and rather muscular, has a quick energetic manner, and a resolute promptness of movement which indicated marked decision and firmness of character. The extraordinary stories by Mrs Gaskell of his inflammable temper, of his burning silk dresses belonging to his wife which he did not approve of her wearing, of his sawing chairs and tables, and firing off pistols in the back-yard by way of relieving his superfluous anger, find no warrant certainly in his present appearance, and are generally considered exaggerations. I remarked to him that I had been agreeably disappointed in the face of the country and the general aspect of the town, that they were less sombre and repulsive than Mrs Gaskell's descriptions led me to expect. Mr Nicholls and Mr Brontë smiled at each other, and the latter remarked: 'Well, I think Mrs Gaskell tried to make us all appear as bad as she could.' Mr Brontë wears a very wide white neck-cloth, and usually sinks his chin so that his mouth is barely visible over it. This gives him a singular expression, which is rendered still more so by spectacles with large round glasses enclosed in broad metallic rims. Though over eighty years old and somewhat infirm, he preaches once every Sunday in his church...As I rose to take my leave Mr Nicholls asked me to step into the parlour and look at Charlotte's portrait. It is the one from which the engraving in the *Life* is made; but the latter does no justice to the picture, which Mr Nicholls said was perfect likeness of the original. I remarked that the engraving gives to the face, and especially to the eyes, a weird, sinister, and unpleasant expression which did not appear in the portrait. He said he had observed it, and that nothing could be more unjust, for Charlotte's eyes were as soft and affectionate in their expression as could possibly be conceived.

PART II

THE COMING OF JOHN WADE: 1861 AND AFTER

Patrick Brontë died on 7 June 1861, at the age of 84, having served Haworth as its pastor for forty years. Tragically for him he had outlived his wife and six children, but his successor, John Wade, was still blessed with a family around him and he soon found the parsonage too small. The large gabled wing on the north side was added in 1878 by which time a number of changes inside the house had already been made.

From the start Mr Wade rarely permitted visitors to intrude upon the privacy of the house and he also discouraged the idea of the church becoming a shrine. When after some years a wealthy parishioner offered to contribute substantially towards the cost of a new church he quickly accepted.

The proposed destruction of the ancient church (the tower alone was spared), which William Grimshaw had enlarged in 1755, caused widespread consternation. Wade had the support of the Bishop of Ripon, following a favourable Consistory Court decision, but in literary circles both at home

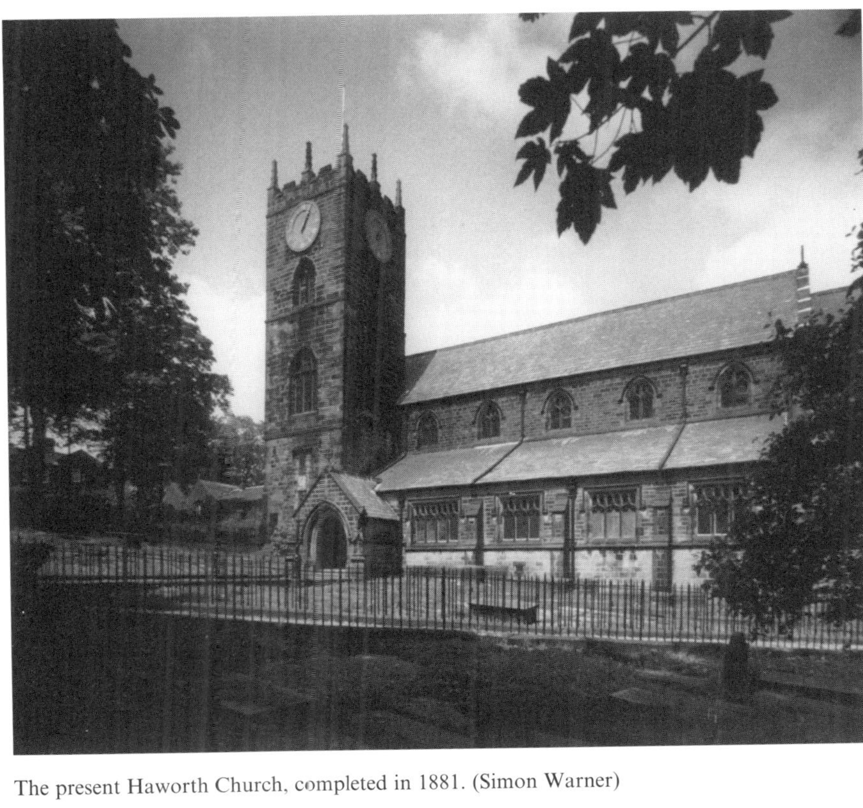

The present Haworth Church, completed in 1881. (Simon Warner)

and abroad opposition was firm and vociferous. Wade was quoted as saying he was 'the best abused man in Yorkshire' but he persisted and the last service in the old church was held on 14 September 1879. The new church, 'ready-made Gothic' as someone described it, was completed in 1881.

Years later, in 1895, the *Times-Star* in far away Cincinnati reported:

> Only the tower of the old church now remains. Otherwise the church has been torn down and rebuilt at the dictation of the present vicar. He said that the church was unhealthy; that the bodies buried under the floor made it a deathtrap; that it was ill-smelling and redolent with poisonous vapours. The press opened its vials of wrath as letters and telegrams came to him; antiquarians protested; churchmen ridiculed. It was asserted by some that the vicar (direct successor of the Rev. P. Brontë) felt himself irrevocably in the Brontë shadow and believed his identity so entirely lost that he desired to efface every vestige of the occupying Brontës.

16

An American Visitor at Haworth: Charles Hale, 1861

Brontë Society *Transactions* 15 Pt 2 126 (1967)

It was on a day in 1967 that a package arrived at the Parsonage containing a photocopy of a sixty-page letter, dated 11 November 1861, started at the Black Bull and completed three days later at the home of Mrs Gaskell.

The writer of the letter was Charles Hale (1831–1882). He was en route to visit his friend W. S. Thayer, U.S. Consul-General in Egypt. Hale had broken his journey in England and was staying with the Gaskell family to whom he had been introduced by his brother Edward, a Unitarian minister and writer friend of the Gaskells.

Charles Hale succeeded his friend Thayer as Consul-General in Cairo in August 1864 but because of ill-health returned to Boston in 1871 and was immediately elected to the State Senate. In 1872 he became Assistant Secretary of State but in 1876 he suffered a breakdown through overwork and died in 1882 at the age of 51.

The copy of Hale's letter to his mother, which is now in the Hale Family Papers, Sophia Smith Collection, Smith College, Northampton, MA, U.S.A., came to Haworth through the courtesy of Mrs Fredson Bowers of Charlotteville, Virginia, a great-niece of the writer.

The letter reads as follows:–

> Here I am in the public room of the Black Bull – the inn which poor Branwell Brontë frequented – about to eat my supper off a tray that belonged to Charlotte Brontë! I left Carlisle by the express train at 1.51 and reached Keighley (117 miles) at 5.22 p.m. There was a fly at the station but Mrs Gaskell had advised me to walk – the fact is that the hill at the end of the road, in Haworth, is so steep that a

horse can't very well get up. A little Yorkshire boy, who approached, I allowed to relieve me of my bag – he said he could go as far as 'the bar' which is just outside Keighley. He said his name was James Robinson – he works in the mills and has lost his left thumb (as I saw) by an accident there – which made it hard for him to relieve himself by a change of his load from right hand to left. I left umbrella and rug at the post office, bought some gloves and shawl-pin at a shop, had the man fasten my shawl tightly about my neck, dismissed my guide at the bar with a shilling, which made him very happy, and plunged out into the darkness. The road however was plain enough and I met lots of people of whom I asked the way from time to time, and found I was going right. There are mills all about here. I think it was in all respects best to walk for there was a good hard sidewalk nearly all the way, and the roadway was pretty muddy – heavy for horses – besides, I was about to say, the great advantage of my walking up was this; that just at the foot of Haworth hill (which Mrs Gaskell describes capitally in her book – seeming at the end almost like a stone wall across the road, with its pavement, it is so steep) – I fell in with two women, of whom I inquired the way to the Black Bull – they said it was directly at the top of the hill, but there was a footpath less precipitous than the road (footpath steep enough as it proved!) which they were going to take and I had best accompany them. So I joined them, and of course we at once fell into conversation. They had both known the Brontës – all of them; the older woman, very long; the younger woman turned out to be the sexton's wife. They talked most pleasantly about them; about Charlotte, her kindly ways, her diminutive stature and silent movements. The sexton's wife told me she had the little wicker-work doll's cradle mentioned in one of the books, and the next day she showed it to me. This talk beguiled the tedious ascent at the end of my walk and seemed fairly to introduce me to living memories of the Brontës. The sexton's wife showed me the Black Bull and I entered.

I found in the public room a blazing fire, the warmth of which was most acceptable. Here too was a young engineer who proved to be a most agreeable person – for they are surveying a railway to connect Haworth with Keighley so that future worshippers will find their pilgrimage easier. While my supper was getting ready I began to write as above. Presently it was brought in, upon the tray which belonged to Charlotte Brontë, and I fell to with zest – for it was my dinner as well. I had been prepared to find the inn accommodation very poor – and was agreeably disappointed in my fare which was by no means despicable.

Well you see a mighty change is going on in Haworth. The last personal trace of the Brontës connection of nearly half-a-century with the place, is vanishing, in Mr Nicholls's removal, about three weeks ago, to Ireland. A new incumbent has been appointed, a Mr John Wade of Bradford, who is very much liked. Mr Nicholls was exceedingly unpopular. He certainly had a strange feeling which one may understand but by no means justify about his wife's separate reputation – He hated that she should be remembered in any other relation than as his wife; as an author or as the chief personage of Haworth he could not bear to have her thought of. The sexton, Mr Brown, determined to name his little girl born six weeks after Mrs Nicholls's death, 'Charlotte Brontë Brown' after her. Mr Nicholls flatly refused to christen the child by that name – so she went unchristened a long time during which she had an illness which might have been fatal, and her parents were much concerned lest she should die without the ceremony which their faith makes important. Old Mr Brontë heard of the circumstance, and taking advantage of a temporary absence of his curate, he sent for the child, and although himself more than eighty years old and released from ordinary parochial duties he christened her by the name her parents had selected and entered it in full in the church register. Mr Nicholls returned, and all seemed well, but the next child that was christened by him caused him to open the register where he saw of course the obnoxious entry; he flew into a violent passion, bounced out of the church, and rushed to old Mr Brontë whom he scolded well. But the old man is believed to have made good his defence – told his curate that he (Mr N.) would have had a very serious thing to answer for to the Bishop if the child had died unchristened, owing to his refusal for no proper reason to perform the ceremony.

But you may imagine how this incident affected the proper estimate of the two clergymen. Mr Brontë was sincerely and truly loved. The sexton said he was the most truly kind and considerate man, while Mr Nicholls he added was just the opposite in all respects. Mr Nicholls threatened the law against the farmers for alleged neglect in maintaining the flagstones across several fields on the path leading from the back of the parsonage to the moors. The sexton, by the way, did not tell me this story about his child's christening, but Mrs Gaskell – I saw the child however and kissed her for her name* ...

After or during tea the sexton and the joiner – the former William Brown and the latter William Wood -came in – the landlord was invited to join us, with the engineer, and we spent the evening until a late hour in talk of the Brontës whom the two Williams had known very well from first to last. William Brown's aunt was the 'old Tabby', the singular servant and housekeeper.

In all the talk of the Brontës, however, it is very singular how all these people at once diverge from the girls to Branwell, although acknowledging his despicable character, his profligacy and its deplorable incidents and consequences ...

While insensibly recording the first place in their admiration to Branwell, these men of humbler station had only good to say of the young ladies – of Charlotte, of Emily and of Anne – the two latter so shy ('shamefaced' is the Yorkshire term) – that they seldom or never spoke to any of the people; but Charlotte would do this whenever there was occasion, although she too was reticent and reserved. They told me a capital story of Emily's bravery in bringing their big dog out of a fight with another dog when no man of all who stood around durst interfere to prevent the savage struggle that was going on.

The sexton has his own portrait painted by Branwell** – and the joiner has three pictures of his to which the following singular and interesting story attaches:

He is cabinet maker as well as joiner and really makes very nice furniture of valuable woods. One time Charlotte had set her heart on something in his shop which she desired for the better furnishing of the house: I thought Brown said a mirror***, but this seems hardly characteristic. After a while, Mr Brontë consented to the purchase and the article was sent for and delivered. The price was five guineas.

* There are some errors here. The child in question was a boy, not a girl, and he was a son of the Greenwoods, not the Browns. The child was baptised 'Brontë Greenwood' on 14 November 1859 as recorded in the Register of Baptisms. I am grateful to Dr Juliet Barker for this information from her book *The Brontës* (Weidenfeld and Nicolson, London, 1994).

** It is now in the Parsonage. See page 26.

*** The 1861 Bill of Sale mentions mirrors.

Now Branwell had been sent to study (or 'apprenticed' as they said here) with an artist of Leeds named Bradley*; and under the eye and with the assistance of his master he had executed three oil paintings: one representing 'Jacob's Dream' and two others. These his father had purchased of the master for the price of ten guineas. Accordingly when the joiner went to the parsonage to get his money (or 'brass' as they say here) he found Mr Brontë and Charlotte sitting by the new piece of furniture and the father told him he would give him these three pictures, which had cost ten guineas, in payment of his bill for five.

Our simple joiner of course was somewhat disconcerted at this proposition, which would pay him with something that he could not but regard as nearly worthless to him and would have refused point

'Jacob's Dream'. Copy in oils (c. 1834–1838) by Branwell Brontë. Based on Genesis 28:10–22 recording Jacob's dream of a ladder from earth to heaven on which angels are seen ascending and descending.

* John Bradley was a Keighley artist and a founder member of the Keighley Mechanics' Institute. He gave lessons to all the Brontë children.

blank; but Charlotte ('Charlotty' he always said: three syllables) looked at him so pleadingly that he held his peace until presently Mr Brontë went out of the room saying: 'Well you may do just as you please; you may take away your mirror (or whatever it was) or you may take away Branwell's three paintings. Suit yourself, I have nothing more to say.'

Then Charlotte said, 'Now, William, please take the pictures and I will make it up to you some time.' So his heart softened and he went away with the pictures; 'though I felt like a fool' said he 'as I came down the lane, to come back with three pictures not worth a sixpence instead of brass that I expected.' But Charlotte did make it up to him – for when she became famous and rich she gave him an order to renew the furniture of the house from top to bottom throughout with his own make. And since her death and Branwell's he has been offered a very large sum (I think fifty guineas) for the paintings, but he will not sell them at that price.*

He told me with some pride parenthetically that the rocking chair which he made for Mr Brontë as a part of this refitting of the house was so good that it sold at the sale for three times its first cost to the Brontës.

This reminds me that I have omitted to mention that Mr Nicholls in going away took nearly everything of especial value or interest which had belonged to his wife; but the remaining household effects were disposed of by public auction about three weeks ago. The sale was considered a matter of no consequence; it was not widely advertised nor largely attended. Yet I would like to have been present – and Mrs Gaskell very much regrets that she was not informed of it. For of all these things I am the bearer to her of news about Haworth.

I suppose the tray I have mentioned was obtained at the sale – the only other article I know of in particular is a copy of Goldsmith's *History of England*, four volumes in one,** which all the Brontë family used; having ms. notes by the father and Wood says by Charlotte also

* Of the three pictures concerned in this curious deal, 'Jacob's Dream' is now in the Parsonage. It is a copy of an engraving by E. Goodall of an original painting by W. Allston. It was presented to the Society in 1894 by William Law, who stated that he had bought it from 'a man named Wood' who had acquired it at the sale after Mr Brontë's death, contradicting Hale's story. (*The art of the Brontës* by Christine Alexander and Jane Sellars, Cambridge University Press 1995). It was still in Wood's possession in 1871. See p. 106.

** Oliver Goldsmith (?1730–1774). His *History of England* was published in 1771. See also page 106.

but I did not happen to see any of hers in turning over the pages. He knows he has seen her using the book and he bought it for eighteen pence. I would gladly have given as many shillings to be possessed of it – and many persons, I dare say, would have been willing to count the price in guineas.

But I am still running away from my narrative. I need not say we had a merry evening – decorous and quiet, of course, but full of pleasant incident. I retired to rest in a very good bedroom, an immense mahogany four-poster bed, with heavy curtains. very high, a little staircase of mahogany carpeted, being provided to get into bed with*. The sheets were clean and the covering ample. Altogether one might find a very much worse place to pass the night in than the Black Bull at Haworth…

Saturday, November 9, 1861

I rose at sun-rise! No great feat however when the sun doesn't rise until between seven and eight. While breakfast was preparing and for about half an hour afterwards, I employed myself in copying some extracts out from an old copy belonging to Brown of a book written and published in 1818 by Mr Brontë called '*The Maid of Killarney, or Albion and Flora: a modern tale in which are interwoven some cursory remarks on religion and politics*'…

When I had finished the sexton came by appointment at about nine o'clock to conduct me to the places I wished to see. I first went to his house where I saw the cradle, the portrait of himself and his little girl. I then went to the church. I entered by the door by which Charlotte usually entered and walked round to her pew – sat a moment where she sat. She used to have a footstool necessarily under her feet, the seat was so high and she so petite – this as well as the carpets, cushions and all fixtures of the pew Mr Nicholls has carried away. The pews are marked with distinct signs painted upon them 'This pew belongeth to so-and-so', 'John Jones hath four seats in this pew.' The pulpit is three desks, one below another, connected by a stair. I ascended to the uppermost which is covered by a sounding board…

The tablet to the Brontës is a new and handsome one. There was not room upon the old tablet to record Mr Brontë's name, so numerous had been the deaths in the family. Mr Nicholls caused the old tablet to be broken into small pieces and buried in the garden of the parsonage. Mrs Gaskell says he broke it up himself with a pickaxe. The sexton

* This room and its remarkable bed figure in two later accounts. See pages 99 and 115.

THE HOME OF CHARLOTTE BRONTE

J. GREENWOOD, STATIONER, &c., HAWORTH.
(By permission of the Proprietors of the London Journal)

England
At Mrs Gaskell's, Manchester,
Monday Morning Nov. 11. 1861

Dear Mother — I have been to Haworth "the home of Charlotte Bronte" as you see by this sheet of paper which I got there. — I had a

The first page of Charles Hale's letter written on the notepaper sold by John Greenwood. The marked upper window is that of Charlotte's bedroom.

did not say that, but he told me the rest and showed me where it was buried. He also showed me where the two dogs were buried in the garden.

In the vestry of the church, being Saturday, the poor were receiving the dole to which they are entitled from the poor rates. The person making the payments was Mr Greenwood, the lovely little stationer of Haworth, whose name is printed on the first sheet of this paper. I saw him afterwards at his shop. He says Charlotte Brontë was the best friend he ever had.

I next went to the parsonage. Here a great transformation is going on. The house is a hundred years old and is sadly out of repair, for Mr Brontë disliked to have mechanical work going on there. Only once, from absolute necessity, to keep out bad leakage, he allowed the roof to be mended. The new incumbent does not choose to go into a rotten old house, but they are doing very much more than making merely necessary repairs. They are putting in fireplaces and mantlepieces of marble, and windows of plate glass, a single pane filling the whole sash and weighing thirty pounds. The stone walls, stone floors of the passages and stone staircases will stand unchanged for another hundred years as they have the last – but the masonry is new pointed and the house will be refitted anew throughout. In old Tabby's chamber for some reason, half the window had been walled up with a stone wall by Mr Brontë's direction; this erection has been pulled down. Mr Nicholls having neglected to bury these stones I might have brought one to America had they not been too heavy. I easily obtained however some very good memorials. I purchased of the proper person the whole lower sash of the window of the bedroom of Charlotte Brontë. This is the window at which she was most fond of sitting. So they all agreed at Haworth and Mrs Gaskell confirmed the statement absolutely. I have marked this window in the engraving. The panes of glass were cut out under my own eye. I also brought away myself plenty of the moulding or woodwork that went about the rooms, so I can frame photographs with wood and glaze them with glass from the place – we shall look at them through the same medium through which Charlotte Brontë saw the dreary landscape before her window and they will be surrounded with wood that was about her as she sat there. I have also the wire and crank of Mr Brontë's bell-pull, which he used daily for forty-one years. The joiner here has a peculiar plane with which he makes alumets or lamp lighters, cutting off the chip and twisting it into shape with one movement of the tool, so they are made quickly. I let him make me a number of these out of wood from the parsonage: some of them I made myself. Such memorials I know will be valued by myself and my friends, besides the photographs which I was able to get of the sexton and of the stationer . . .

Then we walked out on the moor – the favourite walk of all the Brontës. The sexton told me that the moor stretched away nearly twelve miles without interruption of any sort. I supposed this must be an exaggeration, but I find by the reduced ordnance map that the remark is almost precisely true. Mr Brontë used to be seen to walk out to a certain place; stop, look around him gazing; turn on his steps and return. We walked out first on a sort of hill-side above a little valley made by the 'beck' of which the waterfall stream is a tributary. To all these things there are frequent allusions in their books. By and by we came to what is called the Brontë waterfall. It is three or four miles from the parsonage – very wild and picturesque.

Returning from my walk I went to the joiner's to see his treasures. I saw the three pictures by Branwell which he acquired in the manner I have already mentioned, and also the Goldsmith's History which he got at the sale. He has also a pencil sketch by Emily Brontë of early date, of a girl and a dog, with her name in juvenile letters; and a sketch by Charlotte of a goddess with a diadem and harp – Minerva? He would not part with these for any consideration. He considers himself (and justly I think) the most familiar with the Brontës of any of the Haworth people – he is a jolly, frank, honest agreeable man.

Next I went to Greenwood's the stationer. He is mentioned in the *Life*, in a letter of Charlotte Brontë's to her publishers, describing him as a person who wrote an essay on *Jane Eyre* when it first appeared. He aspires to more culture than the rest: is a quiet gentlemanly person: I wish I could have had more talk with him. He has two nice india ink drawings by Charlotte; carefully preserved; one of them is marked in Mr Brontë's handwriting: 'This was drawn by my daughter Charlotte Brontë. P. Brontë, Incumbent of Haworth.' He has also a flower painted in water colours by her, very pretty and nicely framed. He has a presentation copy of Mr Brontë's Poems – and his things seem to be more cherished than any of the others.

These things seen, I took up the line of march back to Keighley. I had some freight to convey in rather bad shape – but I stuffed my coat pockets and wore my coat – strapped my bag across my shoulder and carried my shawl folded across my bag; carried in my right hand the parcels of glass and photographs tied together, and could have carried the timber in the left hand; but Wood the joiner accompanied me and kindly relieved me of that. He had made (for his day's work on the parsonage repairs) a wooden model of the weights required to hang the new plate-glass sashes and was carrying said model to the iron foundry in Keighley to be cast. This, by the way, is how I learned the weight in pounds of the glass. Thus I had a long full talk with Wood, as I had previously had on the moor with Brown. If either of those men know anything about any of the Brontës which I did not acquire, I think I must need a new leather for my pump: it seemed however to draw very well.

I felt pretty tired and heavily-laden before I got to Keighley. Wood kindly took the glass also a part of the time. I was glad enough to see the 'bar' which however is nearly a mile from the railway station. Wood said that if I would stop with him at the foundry while he transacted his errand there, he would then go with me to the station. I gladly acceded to this kind proposal. So I saw the inside of a Keighley iron foundry. At Manchester, Keighley, Haworth etc., in the mills and foundries no work whatever is done on Saturday afternoons, so work was stopped but we found the foreman. He promised to have the weights done on Tuesday morning. At the station I found a train would start in half an hour; leaving my things with an old woman, who was the only living person about the premises, I started back into the town of Keighley to the post office, where I recovered my umbrella and rug, and found a kind letter from Mrs Gaskell telling me to come to her house. I took the omnibus from the Devonshire Arms* back to the station (bidding good-bye to Wood) and arrived just at the right time to take the train.

By the way, the late Duke of Devonshire called on Mr Brontë near the close of their respective lives (I believe the Duke who called is dead**). His carriage was driven all the way up the steep street, producing a noise and profound sensation in Haworth. It even drove up by the church to the very door of the parsonage garden. The Duke alighted and entered the house. Presently his servant returned to the carriage and took into the house a bottle of choice wine in

* This hotel still stands opposite the parish church but has been renamed.

** William George Spencer, 6th Duke of Devonshire, visited Mr Brontë in August 1857 and died the following year at the age of 83. In a letter, Mr Brontë described the visit as 'a token of respect for the memory of the dead.'

which it is supposed they drank each other's healths; and after a while the Duke came out leaning on Mr Brontë's arm and entering his carriage drove away.

...And so ended this most delightful experience...It is now nearly midnight and I close this up for the *Etna* from Liverpool on Wednesday. I shall doubtless receive tomorrow my letters that came by the *Arabia* from Boston, Oct. 30.

Very much love to all
From Charlie

Hale's letter is a remarkable record of devotion to the task which, however pleasurable, he had set himself. One is left wondering what became of the relics he collected during his stay in Haworth. They could still be stored away, forgotten in some corner.

The letter reflects much of what Hale had been told by Mrs Gaskell but it is questionable whether his statement that John Greenwood the stationer was mentioned in the *Life* came from her.

Charlotte's letter, quoted by Mrs Gaskell in this connection was written to W. S. Williams on 19 March 1850* and the relevant passage reads:–

I enclose for your perusal a scrap of paper which came into my hands without the knowledge of the writer. He is a poor working man of this village – a thoughtful, reading, feeling being, whose mind is too keen for his frame, and wears it out. I have not spoken to him above thrice in my life, for he is a Dissenter, and has rarely come in my way. The document is a sort of record of his feelings, after a perusal of *Jane Eyre*; it is artless and earnest; genuine and generous. You must return it to me, for I value it more than testimonies from higher sources. He said, 'Miss Brontë, if she knew he had written it, would scorn him': but, indeed Miss Brontë does not scorn him; she only grieves that a mind of which this is the emanation, should be kept crushed by the leaden hand of poverty – by the trials of uncertain health, and the claims of a large family...

Neither Charlotte nor Mrs Gaskell revealed the name of the 'poor working man'. What Charlotte does write about him, however, in no way tallies with what is known about the 'lovely little stationer' who told Hale that she was 'the best friend he ever had'. That statement is lent authority by Albert Preston in his *John Greenwood and the Brontës*, published in Brontë Society *Transactions* in 1951, where it is stated that Greenwood was as intimate with

* SHB III 88.

the Brontës as anyone outside the family circle and that Charlotte once remarked to Mrs Gaskell that John Greenwood was the one friend she had in Haworth.

Furthermore, it was Greenwood the stationer who met and corresponded with Mrs Gaskell. He was also the man who, on Mr Brontë's orders, set out for Brookroyd one day in July 1850 to enquire about Charlotte. Subsequently Charlotte wrote* to Ellen Nussey:–

> Just at the foot of Bridgehouse hill I met John Greenwood – staff in hand, he fortunately saw me in the cab – stopped and informed me he was setting off to Brookroyd by Mr Brontë's orders to see how I was – for that he had been quite miserable ever since he got Miss Nussey's letter – I found on my arrival that papa had worked himself up to a sad pitch of nervous excitement and alarm in which Martha and Tabby were but too obviously joining him – I can't deny but I was annoyed; there really being small cause for it all.

It is possible that another John Greenwood wrote the essay. It was and still is a very common name around Haworth – the current telephone directory contains over four columns of Greenwoods.

* SHB III 123.

17

A Visit to Haworth in 1866 by Emily Dowson

Brontë Society *Transactions* 15.Pt 3.255 (1968)

The sexton at Haworth once again figures prominently in the account by Emily Dowson (1844–1929) of her visit in September 1866. She was 22 at the time, the younger daughter of Christopher Dowson, of Limehouse, and Mary Domett. The latter's brother and Christopher Dowson were introduced to each other by Robert Browning. Emily had three brothers; the poet Ernest Dowson was a nephew of hers.

It was Emily Dowson's grand-daughter, Miss Mary Secretan, a member of the Brontë Society, who submitted the account in 1968 for publication in *Transactions.*

Accompanied by three female companions Emily Dowson travelled by rail from London on Saturday, 1 September 1866. A few days later the party set off for Haworth, calling en route on Mrs Sidgwick, who had employed Charlotte Brontë as a governess at Stonegappe for a few months in 1839. She was the daughter of John Greenwood a wealthy cotton spinner, who lived at Knowle House, Keighley, a substantial dwelling in its own grounds which still stands. Her marriage to John Benson Sidgwick took place at Keighley Parish Church on 10 January 1827, the ceremony being performed by Patrick Brontë's old friend Hammond Roberson*.

It was in the 1850s that the couple moved to West Riddlesden Hall, which had been acquired by John Greenwood in 1809. John Benson Sidgwick died in 1872; Mrs Sidgwick continued to live at the Hall until she died in 1887.

West Riddlesden Hall is described in *Chronicles and Stories of Old Bingley* by Harry Speight, published by Elliot Stock, Paternoster Row, London, in

* I am again grateful to Dr Barker for this information.

The Knowle, Keighley. The family home of Mrs Sidgwick (née Greenwood).

1898, as occupying a pleasant and well-sheltered position on the north side of the valley above the canal, about a mile from Keighley Station and three miles from Bingley. Most of it was built in 1687 but some additions were made by the Greenwoods.

Monday, 10th. To this day had I been greatly looking forward as that fixed for the expedition to Haworth. The morning was bright and pleasant and our usual fly driver John Ramsay and two horses soon took us up. We bowled along towards Keighley, where Aunt and Jessie went to call on Mrs Sidgwick, who lives in a picturesque house called West Riddlesden Hall. With Yorkshire hospitality she begged us all (including young Platt, whom we had taken on the coach box) to come in to lunch, but knowing a long drive before us, we refused and soon left Keighley behind us.

The village of Haworth is composed of one very long, narrow, steep, stony street, houses and small shops on each side, reminding my friends of Clovelly, [!], giving one uncomfortable, pent-up sensations. The general dreary impression was heightened by our meeting in that short walk two hopeless idiots, one a grinning boy, the other an old man blaring through a tin funnel like a trumpet. Having left this rather

West Riddlesden Hall, Keighley. Mrs Sidgwick's residence at the time of Emily Dowson's visit.

sickening sight behind us, we soon reached the Black Bull, that too well-known hostelry, but leaving that for a later visit we went through the densely filled churchyard to a small gate which took us into the road opposite the schools. A little way up stood the rectory house, with the churchyard all around it, with the exception of this side close to the road. At the garden gate we looked in and saw the small square garden and the thorn trees which Charlotte had planted and tended to carefully. We noticed the cold white door (universal in Yorkshire), the windows of the parlour, the library, the bedrooms, the little nursery over the door where those wonderful children played. We next peeped into the back gate and looked in at the kitchen door in which the Brontës baked, ironed and studied German or as children sat by the fire and talked of their heroes and fancied themselves in fairy islands while the wind howled round them.

The bitterness of winter was confirmed by the servants who came out and spoke to us, one a merry Yorkshire lass who shuddered as she spoke of the wintry weather, and the other a weird cadaverous woman who had known the Brontës and been in Charlotte's class at the Sunday School. We asked where the sexton lived who would show us over the

Parsonage and Churchyard, c. Summer 1860 or 1861. The front door appears to be painted white as described by Emily Dowson but it is not painted white in the photograph on p. 9. It is white to-day.

church; he soon appeared and proved to be a most remarkably intelligent man who not only knew the Brontë family intimately but was truly attached to them and as interested in telling us about them as we were in hearing – and more than this could not be said.

In the churchyard we saw the grave of old Tabby, the faithful nurse and noticed many names, such as Murgatroyd, Pighills, etc. which are familiar to us from *Shirley*. We then entered the church which is of a most curious kind with its plaster ceiling and roof, the old high pews and pulpit and one old pew like an isolated piece of gallery belonging to the lord of the manor, but what struck us was a gallery running along the east end of the church which not only left scarcely standing room within the communion rails below but blocked up the window, the part of which that remained visible being veiled by a green venetian blind. All the pews had their owners' names and a mention of the number of seats belonging to each. One possesses the peculiarity of having 'three seats and a half'. Our guide showed us the large square pew of the Brontës, left as they left it, with its green baize seats and worn hassocks, and the corner seat with its back to the pulpit where Charlotte (or as he called her Charlotta) sat; we particularly noticed the tablets opposite the pew which contained a long list of local dignitaries and the charities to which they subscribed or had founded.

Among them one Pighills left 10/- a year to a school where boys were to be educated and dressed in blue. We pictured how Sunday after Sunday her eyes must have wandered over these dreary details, her mind full of strange and wondrous thoughts.

The sexton spoke of them all as Charlotta, Emily, Anne and Branwell till they ceased to be shadows of the past, but stood before us in vivid colouring as living realities. He told us in simple and graphic words (which we gathered up with eagerness) of the almost supernatural genius of Branwell and we quite shuddered at the description of this uncanny creature with his dwarf-like figure and bushy red hair and by the way he by turns taught and terrified the village boys. He related one anecdote illustrating his extraordinary powers, that on one occasion when he was station master, being hurried over some necessary letter writing, two important letters remained to be written before the next train came in. The train was in sight, so Branwell, seizing two sheets of paper and two pens, sat and wrote two letters at the same time on two entirely different subjects. This he did another time for a bet among some drinking companions at the Black Bull.

Our guide spoke with great affection of Charlotta, who was evidently his favourite of the sisters. 'Emily,' he said 'was taller and more prepossessing like and less melancholy.' Anne he briefly described as 'a nice little thing.' We looked with deep interest at the tablet containing the long list of names, the poor mother, the six children, and lastly the poor old father after all his bereavements. We had a strongly cherished opinion that the father was a harsh, disagreeable man, but the sexton, in a simple and truly polite way said 'It is not for me to contradict you, but if you felt as I do, you would speak differently.'

We went into the vestry and he showed us the 'marriage lines' as he called it, and we saw the signatures of Charlotte, her husband, Arthur Bell Nicholls, her friend E-- (so often spoken of in her *Life*) and Miss Wooler, the faithful old governess [*sic*]. He told us that for a long time Mr Brontë would not consent to their engagement and for three years Mr Nicholls went to a curacy several miles off. They corresponded during that time and at the end of the three years the marriage took place. Our guide told us that it was so quietly arranged that scarcely anyone knew when it was to be and as he described it, 'they bobbed in and out of church until the little party was assembled.'

They stayed at the old Haworth rectory till the day came when she was laid under the stone close to the Communion rails in the old

> church and there the last of the six fragile children faded from their father's house and the old square pew was bereft of the little figure that sat so many years in the one corner seat.
>
> Having bought some photographs and seen some very ancient sacrament cups belonging to the Rev. Grimshaw, a rector of fame many years ago, we parted with our sexton friend with much regret and walked through the churchyard and took the narrow path that led to a stile – impassable we thought to all but the thin figures of the Brontës – on to the moors, where as children they walked together and again the two sisters discussing their books and still later the last sister walked sadly alone. We turned our backs indescribably imbued with the spirit of the scene and returned to the Black Bull and sat and rested in the little parlour close to the door...
>
> After a little further chat and waiting while John Ramsay 'put to' we began to walk down the hill, but before we lost sight of the church and house turned and gave a last lingering look behind at those interesting objects, backed by the brown moors. Take away the association and what had we seen? A straggling, dreary village, a lone, gray, square house with a few stunted trees in a small front garden, a remarkably ugly church and a dirty village inn – and yet, compared with them and the peculiar sensations they aroused, the most splendid palace among the most gorgeous scenery would have sunk to nothing.

There is a disturbing air of superiority about these ladies travelling in a two horse carriage with the usual 'fly driver' and 'young Platt' also on the coach box.

As the party walk up to the village they come across two 'hopeless idiots' – no sign of sympathy here. One of the servants who came out at the Parsonage to talk to the visitors is a 'weird cadaverous woman'. They had come to Haworth with a 'strongly cherished opinion that the father was a harsh, disagreeable man' – a view which the sexton, with studied politeness, suggests is incorrect. Haworth is a 'straggling, dreary village,' Grimshaw's church is 'ugly' and the Black Bull 'a dirty village inn.'

In the following account of a visit made about five months later there is a reference to 'two or three excellent inns'. The Black Bull is 'a most comfortable house of refreshment for man and beast'.

18

A Winter's Day at Haworth, January 1867 by W. H. Cooke

St James's Magazine, 1868

This account first appeared some time in 1868 and its lively style makes fascinating reading.

...I had long been anxious to visit Haworth, and on the 22nd January 1867, finding myself in Leeds, I resolved, in company with a literary friend, to carry out our wish into execution. We therefore took the train at Leeds for Keighley, that being the nearest station to Haworth. Keighley is a long, dirty, straggling town on the Leeds and Skipton line of railway. It seems entirely devoted to mills. The distance of Haworth from Keighley is about four miles. The road ascends the whole way, the traveller having on his right a beck (stream) flowing down the valley in which the town of Keighley is situated. The weather, on the occasion of our visit, was intensely cold, the country all around being a foot deep in snow. The road, in consequence of the severity of the frost, was exceedingly slippery, and our walk, therefore, from Keighley to Haworth, was a somewhat laborious one. A railway was then in course of construction from Keighley to Haworth, and has since the time of our visit been opened. My friend and I were, however not permitted to be blessed with its assistance, so had painfully to clamber along the frozen road, which every moment increased in steepness.

As a turn of the road suddenly brought into view the small quiet figures of two young ladies clad in mourning, one almost started, thinking 'Surely these must indeed be they!' But, alas! It is now twelve years since Charlotte Brontë traversed this road for the last time, and nigher twenty since the three Brontë sisters trod it in company. It was indeed to us a saddening thought that every member of that gifted Brontë family has died without leaving a single lineal descendant, so that, save for the possession of their works – which are left as a precious heritage to us from them – the whole family has disappeared from amongst us as completely as if they had never existed.

The people whom we pass on the road stare hard at us, as though strangers were a rarity in this part. Each passer-by, we notice, instead of shoes or boots, wears wooden clogs, which clank noisily as he proceeds on his way. The sky overhead looked heavy and threatening; whilst in every direction, far as the eye could reach, were hills upon hills of sullen outline. By the time the traveller has accomplished two of the four miles which intervene between Keighley and Haworth, he sees the village of which he is in quest, right before him. At first sight Haworth seems literally to be situated amongst the clouds, for the village stands on the side of a steep hill which is crowned at the top by the village church. From the very back of the church rise the wild moors – the clouds and moors seeming in truth almost to merge themselves in one at the back of the sacred edifice. For a short time the road takes a sudden turn and the traveller loses sight of Haworth. Anon, however, the village again comes in sight, the beck is crossed by a stone bridge, and the foot of the village street is reached, up which we slowly climb. We perceived, as we passed the post-office, that visitors were now expected at Haworth, for in the little window were copies of Charlotte Brontë's works; those of her sisters; Mrs Gaskell's *Life of Charlotte Brontë*; also photographs of the Rev. Mr Brontë, and of the church and parsonage.

At length the top of the village is gained. The road suddenly widening here, the visitor enters an open space or oblong, in the midst of which stands the church, and closely abutting upon it are the schools, the sexton's house, and two or three excellent inns. Dinner having been ordered at the Black Bull – the inn patronised, alas! too frequently by Branwell, the gifted and only brother of the Brontë family – we proceeded to view the church. The sexton, a fine, handsome man, of perhaps five-and-thirty years of age, showed us over the church. Unlike most *cicerones* of his class, who immediately the visitor enters begin their sing-song, cut-and-dried, monotonous account of each object of interest, this man waited to be questioned, and when questioned, answered the various inquiries we put to him, quietly and well.

The church is of great antiquity, but it is an ugly, puritanical building, without any pretensions to architectural beauty of any sort. The pulpit, reading-desk, and clerk's seat are all placed one above the other, thus forming what the extreme High Church party, in derision, call 'a three-decker'...

The sexton who is the son of the former sexton*, who presided during Charlotte's life, was born at Haworth, and has lived there all his days.

'Yes, he knew every one of the Brontë family well. No, they didn't visit much among the people in the village. They were fonder of taking long walks by themselves on the moors. Many a time, sir, have I seen them, along with their dogs, going up that path,' pointing, as he spoke, to a narrow foot-road crossing the churchyard, and ascending at once onto the sweeping, snow-covered moors. 'Yes, Emily was very reserved. Anne was the loveliest, sir. Whenever they were baking at the parsonage, she always took care to make me – I was a little lad, then, you know, sir – an apple pasty; or, if she couldn't make me one, then she would give me a handful of raisins, or something of that sort.'

'Did you know Branwell?' said I.

'Oh, yes, I knew him well, too.'

'Was he not very clever ?'

'That he was, sir !'

'Did you know Mr Nicholls, the curate, who married Charlotte Brontë?' asked my friend.

'Yes; I knew him well. A nice man he was. Quiet, you know, but very kind, and a real good hard-worker.'

'How long was Mr Nicholls at Haworth ?'

'Why, altogether, he was here for about seventeen years. Ten years he was here afore he married Miss Brontë, and about seven years afterwards. Four months after Mr Brontë died he went away.'

'Did he apply for the living after Mr Brontë's death?' we asked.

'Yes; he did, sir,' answered the sexton; 'but he didn't get it.'

'But surely,' said we, 'having been curate here for seventeen years of his life, having known the Brontë family so long, and having married Charlotte Brontë, he was the most suitable person to have been appointed.'

'Well, I don't know how it was sir,' responded the sexton; 'but all I know is, he sent in his application to the trustees, and hearing there was going to be some opposition to him, he withdrew it.'**

'Mrs Gaskell was also here, was she not?' inquired my friend.

* Not so. William Brown was the brother of John Brown, who died in 1855.

** This matter is fully dealt with in *The Brontës* by Dr Juliet Barker.

‘Yes, sir,’ replied the sexton, ‘she was here; but we don’t like her nor yet her book. She says something about us folk that isn’t true. We think her book’s libellous.’

So talking, he showed us the communion pew, in front of which Charlotte Brontë was married, and under which she now lies buried, almost on the very spot where her feet must have stood during the performance of the marriage rite. All the family, also, except Anne, are buried close beside her. The sexton then pointed out to us the Brontë pew, which is close before the altar, and especially showed us where she (Charlotte) used to sit.

‘She was,’ he said, ‘very little and had a footstool for her feet. I once saw Thackeray and an American, who, they tell me, is a great man over there, called Emerson, and Miss Martineau, and Miss Brontë, all sitting in that pew one Sunday*. Thackeray and Emerson came to visit Miss Brontë for a day or two, that was how they all sat there on the Sunday’...

Having duly inscribed our names in the visitors’ book, which, we noticed, contained the names of persons from all quarters of the globe, we were taken out of the church into the churchyard and shown the grave of old Tabby, the faithful servant, for thirty years, of the Brontë family, and who loved each member of that family with a mother’s love. Her grave is immediately in front of the parsonage house, which faces down upon the church. It is a plain house, of two storeys in height, and is built of grey stone, in the most substantial manner, in order to enable it to withstand the fierce wintry blasts which sweep down upon it from the desolate moors. The house is roofed with stone tiles, as the wind would easily strip off any ordinary covering of tiles. A small garden, containing a few shrubs, lies in front of the house, separating it from the graveyard.

The present incumbent of Haworth has, with execrably bad taste, removed the plain, old-fashioned house-windows which existed during the Brontës’ time, and has substituted large, bran-new plate-glass ones, of the most approved Regent-street construction. Anything more utterly out of keeping with the rest of the surroundings than are these plate-glass windows it is impossible to conceive. Everything else about the house – always excepting those unfortunate plate-glass windows – is in unison with the weird, desolate scene which surrounds the parsonage.

* This is a flight of fancy.

Standing near Tabby's grave a very fine view may be obtained of the hills and moors which surround the churchyard on every side. The parsonage-house apparently consists of two rooms, one on each side of the door. We say 'apparently consists' for we were not allowed to enter it – the present incumbent sternly refusing to admit a single visitor, or to permit one, even for an instant, to peer into that family sitting-room of the Brontës, wherein were written works which have conferred immortal lustre upon this incumbent's present residence, and which will live long after he himself has mouldered down to dust, and his bran-new window frames have rotted to decay* ...

We thereupon proceeded to the Black Bull to discuss dinner. On entering that comfortable hostelry, we were informed by the attendant damsel that we were to be regaled upon a joint of roast beef, which, she said, had been roasting all that 'nooning,' i.e., forenoon. The Black Bull is the chief inn at Haworth, and, truth to tell, is a most comfortable house of refreshment for both man and beast. The viands are excellent, the attendance good, and the charges moderate. Being ushered into the comfortable parlour – its bright fire and crimson hangings contrasting pleasantly with the snow outside – we were shown a comfortable, old-fashioned round arm-chair, in which our landlady told us that Branwell Brontë had often sat, alas! too long...

After dinner we resolved to take a walk upon the moors, although they were more than a foot deep in snow. Crossing, therefore, the churchyard, we struck into the narrow path which ascends from it on to the moors, and up which, the sexton told us, the Brontë family and their dogs, had so often passed before us.

The path is at first narrow, ascending between two stone walls. An evidence of the bleakness of the place, and consequent want of trees, may be found in the fact that the stiles which cross this path are made of flat slabs of stone. Not a single wooden one could we see. Not the least change has taken place in this road since the Brontë girls last swept up it, nigh twenty years ago. Proceeding perhaps two hundred yards along this path, we reached a point where another road struck off to the right. Presuming that this would lead us right out on to the moors, we followed it, and, sure enough, after two minutes scrambling, we found ourselves right out on the wide spreading moors, and were looking down – despite its elevated position – upon Haworth Church,

* All the plate-glass was removed in 1955 when the windows were restored to their original state.

which lay directly at our feet. The appearance presented by this wide, snow-covered expanse of wide moorland, stretching away in a west-north-west direction, in unbroken continuity, as far as the eye could reach, was very striking. The wind blew across these moors on that January winter's day, fiercely, coldly, but right gloriously. As it hurried past, its music thrilled us and made us feel strong with reinforced strength.

We were rejoiced to see, on reaching the back of the parsonage, that it is left in precisely the same state as when the Brontës occupied the house. No hideous new windows spoil the effect of its weather-worn walls, scarred and marked as they are by the tempests and storms of the last hundred years. There we could still see the old kitchen in which the Brontë girls in their childhood had so often sat; in which, when grown up, they performed their regular round of household duties; in which poor faithful old Tabby, their servant, ministered for so many years to their wants, and 'did the duty which lay nearest her,' in the place God put her.

And as, amid the fast-gathering darkness of that winter's night, we walked back to Keighley, we thought sadly of those lights of genius that had burned so brightly – only a few short years ago – in that lone parsonage-house, situated among the solitary hills.

19

Two Days at the Home of the Brontës by E. P. Evans, 1871

The Treasury of Literature, December 1872

The following is taken from another long-forgotten periodical. The issue is dated 2 December 1872 and relates to a visit made the previous summer. This is a most impressive account. In clear and powerful language the writer produces in the reader's mind a vivid picture of life in Haworth in 1871 at the time of the rushbearing celebrations.

I was obliged to wait two hours for the train on the branch railway to Haworth and spent most of the time in the waiting room with the motherly old attendant, who knew the neighbourhood well, and could tell me much about the family who had made it famous. After leaving Bradford the road passes through several small manufacturing villages, of which Keighley is the most important, and peculiarly interesting to me as having been once the nearest station to Haworth, and the terminus of many a walk of the Brontë sisters. A few miles further on the guard called out 'Haworth' and, after barely giving time for a few passengers to alight, the train passed on, and I was left standing on the platform of the solitary little station at the foot of the hills. I followed the people, and presently accosted a tall, sedate-looking woman who was nearest to me, and asked her as to the prospect of finding a lodging in the village. As soon as she heard that I had come far out of my way to see Haworth she became very cordial, and introduced me to the little company generally, who made me welcome in a simple, hearty fashion, which was very promising, and beguiled for me the exceeding steepness of the ascent. Instead of going by the paved road, we followed a narrow path between stone walls which wound among the fields, so that I was almost in the centre of the village before I recognised its nearness. It is built mainly along one long street, and as we emerged from the high-wall lane I saw all the famous localities at once.

There were the church, the parsonage, the churchyard terribly 'full of upright tombstones'; and beyond these the dim outline of the moors. The little inn of the Black Bull was directly in front of us; but it was not until we came close to it that I observed the house and its surroundings to be as plain as possible, to stand the wear and tear of the crowds of rough-shod country people who were expected to make it their headquarters for the next three days. One little room upstairs, however, had been left undisturbed and that was given to me. It was old-fashioned and queer, and the bed, besides having high posts, was so high itself that a pair of steps stood ready at the head to assist the future incumbent to scale its mountain of feathers.

From my open window I could look across a lane to the Mechanics' Institute – a modest building, containing the village library and a room for reading and debate. The intervening space had been rented for the fair-time by owners of booths for refreshments and fancy articles, a few of which were already in operation; and in the centre had been planted one of those whirligig machines wherein a large number of children go round and round, imagining themselves meanwhile on horseback or in a carriage. Of course, so novel an amusement had greatly aroused the village children, and they stood by in full force while a few of their number, the happy possessors of a halfpenny or so, mounted the machine and flashed by before the envious gaze of their impecunious companions. It was quite an amusing sight; but when speaking of it to the landlady during the good dinner to which I was presently called, she replied that the machine should never be allowed to come there again, for she was 'fairly stalled wi' their noise.' I remembered the Yorkshire expression for fatigue, and could have hugged the good woman for allowing me to hear it in Yorkshire air.

My dinner was served in the private parlour – a pleasant room with an open fireplace and windows looking upon the street, and furnished with a shiny hair-cloth sofa and oak chairs of antique form grown dark and glossy with age. It was the same room to which Branwell Brontë had often been summoned for the entertainment of such travellers as were above the ordinary society of the Black Bull.

After dinner I went out, and, in obedience to my rule of 'business before pleasure' proceeded to secure photographs of the place before beginning my round of personal inspection. One of the shopkeepers was a woman – a fair, plump matron – who had once been a pupil of Charlotte in the Sunday-School. I made the acquaintance of several persons in the course of my shopping, all of whom could give reminiscences of the family; and, though the incidents were mainly the same that I had read, they seemed fresh and new when heard from living lips. One man asked me if the village looked as I had expected to find it. On my answering in the affirmative, he continued, ' but don't you find the people less rough in their manners than Mrs Gaskell has described them?' I could bear willing testimony to their courtesy and kindness so far as I had been brought into contact with them, and made haste to do so, to his evident gratification; for the pride of the inhabitants had no doubt suffered from that strong picture of their local peculiarities. After securing my photographs I started with my mind free to enjoy the experiences that were yet to come. The churchyard adjoins the inn at one corner, and I passed through the great iron gates, which had been opened for a funeral procession. The ordinary entrance is between open posts at the other end of the church, for the enclosure is a thoroughfare, affording a short cut to the farmhouses and moors beyond. None but foot-passengers can enter it, however, as the place is too thickly sown with graves to allow of a carriage road; and the paths, excepting one to the church door, are not well defined, because people wind their way among the tombs or walk upon the huge flat memorial stones to suit their convenience...

In my wanderings among the graves I had reached the upper end of the enclosure very near the parsonage. Of course, my dearest wish had been to enter the house, especially the room where the sisters had been accustomed to sit together, and where the last survivor had so often paced to and fro in the lonely evenings, haunted by the faces that had vanished, and the voices that were silenced for ever.

But I was told that the present rector had positively refused admission to every stranger that had applied; and, in view of the thousands who visit the place, one cannot blame him for asserting his right to domestic privacy. He never knew the Brontë family, and though he takes pride in their fame he cannot be expected to open his house to all who through curiosity, or even a better motive, may wish to see their former haunts. Besides, the gratification would be only partial, if it would not better deserve to be called a disappointment; for the house has been modernised and completely refurnished, and no trace of its former occupancy remains. Even 'the small old-fashioned window-panes' have been exchanged for the light sash and large glass of the present day. It is easy to tell from the outside the arrangement of the rooms, and so there is nothing but the blessed consciousness of having been in the very places made sacred through the habitual presence of those gifted beings.

By standing on a tombstone I could see over the hedge into the front yard; and as I could do this without intrusion I took a long and careful survey of the premises.

There were the massive stone steps which they had daily crossed, and the old-fashioned front door which had closed upon them all one after another as they were carried to their burial. The flower beds under the windows still remained, but the square grass plot was now adorned with a large circular mound flaming with verbenas and scarlet geraniums. The grass was cut close and looked like velvet, and the gravel paths were trim and neat. The place was evidently well cared for; and as I heard the cheerful voices of the rector and his wife, who were at work in the lower end of the garden, and saw the white curtains waving in the summer air through the open windows, I imagined how it might have been during that brief period in Charlotte's experience, when 'the sacred doors of home' were 'closed upon her married life' and 'her loving friends

'... the square grass plot was now adorned with a large circular mound flaming with verbenas and scarlet geraniums...'

This early 20th century photograph reveals that the garden had not changed much since Mr Evans described it in 1871.

standing outside caught occasional glimpses of brightness, and pleasant murmurs of sound, telling of the gladness within.'

Returning towards the church, I found it open, and the sexton's wife sweeping and dusting for the next day's festival, while the sexton was dancing the baby upon a tombstone by the door. Remembering the numerous deaths of children I had seen recorded, I asked the man whether the close proximity of so crowded a graveyard – which is also at a higher elevation than the town – was not injurious to the public health. He admitted that it had been so in past times, when the people used water from the village wells, and found it often 'greasy'; but during a severe epidemic a company of chemists came from London, and, after testing the water forbade its use; since when the inhabitants had brought water from springs found on neighbouring farms above the level of the churchyard.*

Haworth Church is very old. The outside is plain; the windows are large, and filled with common glass in small panes. I noticed in some of these panes a protuberance as large as an egg, and asked the sexton how they came there. He said that the glass was made long ago, before its manufacture had been so well understood as now, and when a defect could not so easily be remedied. He added that each of these protuberances acted as burning-glass, and church-goers were always careful to avoid their vicinity on a sunny day.

The sexton's wife was obviously accustomed to the visits of strangers, and she now proceeded to show me the objects of greatest interest. The interior of the church is quaint and queer enough to eyes accustomed to the regularity of modern church architecture. The pulpit is high, with an umbrella-like sounding-board over it. In front of the pulpit, and a few feet lower down, is the reading desk; and still lower is a little nook for the clerk or other inferior official. But these seats of authority are not at one end of the building, as in some churches, but in the middle of one side, and the pews are built close up to them; while the communion table, enclosed in a small chancel, is at the eastern end.

* On 28 August 1849 a petition, for which Mr Brontë and others had campaigned, was sent to the General Board of Health in London, that urgent action should be taken about the appalling state of the water supply and the lack of proper sanitation in Haworth.

A few residents were fortunate enough to have access to spring water but most drew their supply from wells which were heavily contaminated by the crowded churchyard at the top of the village and the mortality rate exceeded that established by law as unhealthy. After a long delay Benjamin Babbage, a Board of Health Inspector, came to Haworth in April 1850 and as a result of his alarming report the necessary steps were taken to improve the situation.

Interior view of Haworth Old Church

The gallery, broad and low and divided into pews, runs around the other three sides; the organ stands at the eastern end, over the communion table. The pews below are square and high, and divided by two aisles paved with tombstones, for the space underneath the church is full of graves; and after the interment of Mr Brontë it was decided not to allow any more burials there.

The Brontë pew is the last of the pews on the side next the pulpit. There is only a narrow passage between it and the little chancel, and on the wall is the tablet containing the record of the departed family, while under the pavement is the family vault. The pew is cushioned with green moreen*, and remains as formerly, the rector's family preferring a better lighted seat; consequently this one is let to a parishioner, and is often filled with strangers. I asked permission to sit there on the morrow, which was readily granted; and then the sexton pointed out the places once occupied by the sisters – Emily in the farther corner, facing the clergyman, Anne next, and Charlotte by the door. While he was talking I sat down for a few moments in each seat, for fear that I should have no chance the next day.

* A stout woollen, or woollen and cotton material, for curtains, etc.

Haworth Parsonage and Barn seen from the Church tower, 1879.

After leaving the church, I kept on up the street, following the low wall which encloses the churchyard till it rises higher, to form the boundary of the parsonage grounds. I passed the kitchen, which has a separate gate and pathway from the street. The door stood open, and I could hear the rattle of cooking utensils and the merry laughter of a child. Opposite is a substantial stone barn* where chickens were strutting about and cackling in the sunshine. The street, which is more like a quiet lane, ends here, but there is an opening in the stone wall at its head, and a narrow footpath crosses the edge of several fields till it is lost in the moors beyond.

Directly after breakfast the next day I started for a walk upon the moors. It was a fresh, sweet summer morning; the sky was clear, and dewdrops sparkled on the grass. I walked up the street past the parsonage, and took the same path that I had followed the day before. In one of the fields, leaning upon the wall and talking earnestly, were two women, apparently mother and daughter. They gave me a civil 'good morning' as I came up and I stopped and entered into conversation with them. They had both known the Brontë family well, and the young one had been one of Charlotte's pupils. They expressed deep affection for the whole family and especially regretted Charlotte's untimely death so soon after her happy married life had

* Demolished in 1903.

begun, and when there was promise of the perfection of her joy in the immediate future.

After leaving my new acquaintances I went towards the moors. They rose before me, south and west, in an undulating sweep as far as the eye could reach; but towards the north the fields sloped down a broad valley, in which were a few detached houses (the suburbs, as it were, of the closely-built village on the height), and among them the Methodist and Baptist chapels, each with its separate burying ground.

The moors are not what I had formerly supposed them to be – immense tracts of level land covered with short, dry grass – their surface is greatly diversified , and their unevenness, together with the thickness of the heather that grows upon them, makes walking a toilsome process. The general appearance of these wastes is that of a marsh suddenly dried up, only that to the desolation of barrenness is added the dreariness of superior elevation. They are very dreary, very desolate even in summer, when the gorse and heather are in blossom and the air is full of the murmur of bees; they must be bleak indeed when the snow settles upon them and the winter winds sweep over them. And yet there is the charm of freedom in their wild solitude – a charm which impresses even the passing stranger, and which it is easy to imagine must have held strong power over the sensitive minds of the sisters, who had known them from early childhood.

There was no-one in sight at this early hour, and after wandering about till I was tired I sat down upon a mass of heather, and, lulled by the humming of the bees and the otherwise perfect silence of the place, I lost for a time the consciousness of my own identity in trying to realise the daily influences of nature and society that had shaped and disciplined those remarkable characters.

I was roused at last by the ringing of the bells in Haworth Church, answered like an echo by those of another church upon another hillside miles away. On my return, I followed a path which soon left the moors for the highway, and then led through green lanes and by pleasant farms to a stile at the upper end of the churchyard. As I mounted the steps, I thought that never before had I seen so cheerful-looking a burial place. Some anniversary had evidently drawn many visitors to the village, and groups of these, attired in their Sunday's best, sat with their friends upon the flat tombstones, or wandered about reading inscriptions. The church was nearly full when I entered , and the Sunday-school children, in white dresses and blue sashes, made a fine show in the organ gallery. The

Brontë pew was still empty when I took my seat, but soon an old man entered, who, perceiving that I was a stranger, bowed politely and made some slight remark which led to an extended conversation, in which I learned that he had been warden of the church in Mr Brontë's time, and a familiar friend of the whole family. He told me, too, that, being a carpenter, he had made all their coffins. The opening words of the service interrupted our talk, but the old man concluded by inviting me to return with him to his house at its close to see some relics of the family, which I gladly consented to do.

The service was read by the Rector, the Rev. John Wade, and his curate, and the sermon was preached by the Vicar of Kildwick. I was quite surprised at the excellence of the singing; the organ was well played and the children's voices had evidently received careful training. The psalms for the day were chanted in full, and even in the Lord's Prayer and the Creed the organ and choir followed the voice of the rector, sentence by sentence, with soft, sweet melody, and low but distinct articulation. On expressing my surprise afterwards at such proficiency in the school children, I was told that the improvement dated from Mr Nicholls' arrival in the parish as Mr Brontë's curate. Before that time the music had been simple, as one would expect to find it in so remote and small a parish; but he had at once taken the matter in hand, and introduced a portion of the choral service of the cathedrals, to the satisfaction of all concerned.

After service I accompanied Mr Wood to his home, according to agreement. He showed me a full set of the books written by the sisters, which had been presented by Mr Brontë, and contained his autograph, signed only a few days before his death, the recipient having supported him in bed for the purpose. I saw also a small water-colour sketch of a girl playing on a harp, drawn by Emily in early youth. This was nothing more than the crude attempt of a beginner; but an oil-painting of 'Jacob's Dream' by Branwell, which hung upon the wall, was full of promise. Another most interesting object was an old copy of somebody's 'History of England', bound in leather, grown almost black with time, and with copious notes upon its yellow margins in Charlotte's fine, neat handwriting. I was told that this book had been a great favourite with her from childhood, and lay always upon her table till her death. I had hoped to find the original crayon portrait of Charlotte in care of some friend; but I now learned that this picture, together with all her personal property and as much of the furniture as it was practicable to move, was carried to Ireland by Mr Nicholls, who is now living there, and has married his cousin, a Miss Bell. Martha, the devoted servant, accompanied him, so that every living trace of the family has disappeared from Haworth.

The good old man seemed pleased by my interest in what he had to tell, and regretted that he had not something left which had belonged to the sisters to give me. When the household was broken up after Mr Brontë's death a great many articles, of worth only through their associations, such as old pens, scraps of manuscript, etc., were given to him, but these had been begged or carried off by strangers, until now he had saved only one token from each member of the family for his own sorrowful pleasure.

We spoke of Mrs Gaskell's book, and he regretted the misinterpretation of character which had arisen from her eager acceptance of information from any and every source. He said that he had known Mr Brontë intimately from his arrival in the parish till his death, and that his temper was not of a kind to require the occasional discharge of pistols as a safely-valve for the wrath which he would not allow himself to express in words; also, that the story of his having burned up his children's coloured shoes and cut up his wife's silk dress as protests against finery was entirely false and absurd.

His opinion of the children agreed with that of others whom I talked with. Emily was an intellectual wonder, but her sympathies were either deficient, or repressed by over sensitiveness and the unfavourable circumstances of her short and lonely life. Anne was gentle and affectionate, but less remarkable than either of her sisters. Charlotte's character seems to have been the grandest of all, combining as it did great power with conscientious activity and unselfish tenderness. Branwell was a great genius, perhaps the most splendidly gifted of all the group; and his lack of principle, while it must be bewailed, can also be, partially at least, explained and excused by contemplating the ruinous influences upon such a nature of an unoccupied and aimless life in a place so void of mental stimulus and incentives to ambition as Haworth...

On returning to my quarters I found not only the inn, but the churchyard adjoining, and the street in front, crowded with guests, many of whom, I was told, had come to attend the annual 'Rushbearing' which was to begin next day. Of the origin and meaning of this festival I could discover nothing more than is implied in the expression itself It is still held in obedience to long-established custom, but of its former characteristics there remain only the merrymaking and small trading which were probably at first only attendant upon some kind of earnest labour. The landlord, with his wife and pretty, pale-faced daughter, and all the servants besides, were hurrying to and fro preparing an elaborate dinner, which was to be eaten in the hall of the Mechanics' Institute, for lack of room elsewhere. My table, however, was spread in the private parlour of the inn, and the landlady brought me roast duck as an especial treat, there being not enough of that delicacy to set before the famished multitude. My dessert was a pie made of bilberries – a fruit of which I had often read, and which I found, in appearance and flavour, to be something between a whortle-berry and a cranberry.

After dinner I went out again upon the moors, and, finding a secluded spot, lay down in the heather, where I could see nothing but the waste of purple blossoms around me and the blue sky overhead, and bade farewell in my thoughts to the scenes and associations which I had long pictured in imagination and had at last found so pleasant and dear in reality. The church bell again aroused me from my reverie and I returned by the same shady lanes that I had followed in the morning. The view from some points was very fine. There were groves and orchards and fair homesteads in the valleys, and on all sides the undulating outline of the Yorkshire hills, many of them thickly wooded, others cultivated far up the sides in fields where boundaries were perceptible only by the varied colour of their crops. I was agreeably disappointed in the scenery around Haworth. It is indeed wild, and in winter may be oppressively dreary; and presenting a strong contrast to the luxurious and tender beauty of some of the midland and southern counties of England.

The next morning was dark and rainy. I was to leave by the nine o'clock train; and while breakfast was preparing I went out in spite of the storm, and walked up the street past the parsonage kitchen, where I could see once more the windows of the family parlour and Charlotte's room above.

As I passed the church the door was open and I found Mr Wood within, who, with his assistants, was taking down the scaffolding in front of the organ, where the school-children had sat the day before. He told me many little anecdotes of past times – how 'the girls' would often come to his house because they saw so much of him at their own, though in general they were shy of visiting; how Branwell would come to him, and talk for hours of his longing to go out into the great world and see its wonders for himself; how, when Charlotte's portrait came from London, he was sent for without knowing why, and how Charlotte laughed because, not being accustomed to crayon pictures, he did not at first feel sure that it was meant for her.

He spoke well of Mr Nicholls and said that though it took some time for the inhabitants to understand him thoroughly, as he introduced into the management of church and school affairs many improvements which were at first considered merely as innovations, still their prejudices gradually wore away and became in the end quite popular. But the place was too full of mournful associations for him to be contented there, and soon after Mr Brontë's death he returned to his old home and early friends.

My hostess gave me an affectionate good-bye. On the brow of the hill I paused before descending, and turned to take a last glimpse of Haworth. The rain had ceased and the clouds were rolling by in great billowy masses towards the west.

In view of the excitement which pervaded the literary world concerning the writings of the Brontë sisters while their authorship remained a mystery, and the enthusiastic reception of Mrs Gaskell's unique biography, it might seem that at present those writings have begun to relax their hold upon the reading public. But the crowds of strangers, both native and foreign, who every summer flock to Haworth to read for themselves that pathetic record in the little church, and turn away disappointed from the closed door of the parsonage, prove that there still exists a strong interest in the lives that were so sorrowful, and yet so bravely lived.

For Emily and Anne there was short time for performance, though in what they gave there was glorious promise of future achievement; and for Charlotte, too, we can but echo the lament of her friend, 'If she had but lived!'

It was a happy chance that the visit by E. P. Evans coincided with the rushbearing. He provides an interesting account of what must have been an annual highlight in the lives of Haworth people.

Until the 15th century seats were not permitted in churches, by which time the practice of spreading rushes, mingled with sweet herbs, to avoid sitting directly on cold stone floors, was well established. Once a year the rushes were swept out and a fresh supply was put down. It was usually carried out between haytime and harvest. The rushes were cut on the Saturday and carted to the church. After the strewing, the day ended with a feast and celebrations.

A form of rushbearing still persists to-day in some places, more as the observance of an ancient custom than anything else. There is a reference to the practice in *King Henry IV Part II* (V.v.1) where at Westminster three grooms enter bearing rushes.

20

A Pilgrim at Haworth: Sidney Biddell, September 1879 by Ivy Holgate

Brontë Society *Transactions* 14.Pt 1.29 (1961)

Among those protesting against the imminent destruction of the old church was Sidney Biddell, a London barrister and a keen admirer of Charlotte Brontë, who visited Haworth in 1879. He brought with him a copy (now in the Brontë Parsonage Museum) of the 1876 edition of Mrs Gaskell's *Life* and used the margins and blank spaces in that book as a kind of diary.

Ivy Holgate was a well-known Bradford writer and historian, and a member of the Brontë Society's Council, when in 1961 her account of Biddell's stay in Haworth was published in *Transactions:*

In the space above Chapter One of the *Life* Mr Biddell made the first of his pencilled notes:

> Thursday, September 4th, 1879. At the Black Bull, Haworth; room (bed) overlooking the churchyard. 11 p.m.

The next of his notes was made only a few hours later:

> Friday, September 5th, 1879. 5 a.m. My window faces the bottom of the churchyard and is in full view of the eastern end of the church, built thus, two gables, three windows and tower at extreme end of the church.

He visited the church later that morning. In the dimmed interior he halted to read the inscription on the Brontë memorial that was all too soon to be taken down in preparation for the work of demolition. It was probably during those few moments that he conceived the idea of providing a more impressive monument to the memory of the illustrious sisters when the new church was built and reconsecrated. [John Wade had given an undertaking that the Brontë vault should not be disturbed].

The pilgrim wasted no time of his brief sojourn at Haworth. On his first day he called on Martha Brown. Mr Biddell, no doubt, was intent on acquiring some object or manuscript from the old servant.

On page 304 of his book he recorded his visit. Why he chose this page of the *Life* would seem to be that it holds the printed letter Charlotte wrote to Martha from Scarborough, where she remained for those few days following Anne's death and burial. Beneath the printed letter Martha chose to leave her autograph:

> Martha Brown. September 5th, 1879.

Mr Biddell added a footnote:

> I called and was with Martha Brown for three-and-a-half hours. The above is her signature which she wrote for me.

He would have time enough to hear a good deal from the old servant of the sad events and the happy interludes of the Brontë story; and there was time enough to allow for Martha's bringing out from secret places, and shewing to Mr Biddell, those few precious objects which had come into her possession from the Brontës by deed or gift...

Certain marginal jottings throw a little light on that meeting. On page 60 of his book Mr Biddell wrote:

> Martha Brown shewed me one of the little magazines in Charlotte's handwriting. The leaves were enveloped in whitey brown paper and containing some ten or fifteen pages, size about 2 inches by $1\frac{1}{2}$ inches. Full of very small writing, September 1879.

On page 102 of his book, beside Mrs Gaskell's description of a group portrait of the Brontës, done by Branwell – obviously the 'Pillar' portrait, Mr Biddell puts a query in the margin: 'Where is this painting?' We know now, though Mr Biddell in 1879 did not – nor did anyone else, perhaps, save Mr Nicholls – that his painting was hidden away in a cupboard in the latter's house in Ireland...

Turning to the following page we find preserved another of Mr Biddell's relics – one he obviously treasured; it is a letter written to him from Martha wherein she refers to a group painting; it could have been the Gun Group. The letter is dated October 22, 1879:–

71 Ireton Street
Princeville
Bradford

Dear Sir

As you expressed a wish to have my photo when at Haworth I now enclose you one and also a group from the photograph taken from a painting by P.B.Brontë, it was in Bradford at the time you were in Haworth you will remember me speaking about it.

I shall be staying at my sisters at the above address for another week.

I remain yours very gratefully and respectfully,

Martha Brown

Martha's statement: 'it was in Bradford at the time you were in Haworth', if she is referring to a painting, eliminates the Pillar Portrait and seems to give proof that the Gun Group* was in Bradford at this time. It is interesting to note that Mr Horsfall Turner's book *Haworth Past and Present* was in the course of production at this time and the Gun Group appears among the illustrations in the book.

It is a matter for curiosity that Mr Biddell has pencilled out every mention of Mr Nicholls in his book. He had never met Mr Nicholls but he certainly had a deep animosity for Charlotte's husband. His opinion of the marriage appears in the margin of page 445:– 'A most deplorable event'...

The frustration Mr Biddell experienced with regard to the proposed memorial is contained in a letter he wrote to Ellen Nussey: 'I have not the heart to do much in reply to Mr Wade's letters. There is such a wheel within a wheel in everything in connection with Haworth, its Rector** and its new church that I have not the courage to attempt more than a simple memorial cross or plate...'

* Ivy Holgate's assumption that the photograph Martha Brown sent to Biddell was that of the Gun Group was perfectly correct.

** A few years after Mr Brontë's death Haworth Church gained its independence from Bradford. As a result, it was thenceforth a parochial chapelry and John Wade became its first Rector. When Patrick Brontë came to Haworth in 1820 he was appointed by the Church Trustees as its Perpetual Curate and so he remained until his death.

> The brass plate was all he achieved, but his effort to provide something on a grander scale than that simple but dignified brass, was tremendous, costing him time and money. He spent hours on the composition of appeals to known admirers of the Brontës but these he committed to the fire – they never reached the hands and eyes of those to whom he had written them. He visited Charlotte's publishers, Smith, Elder & Co., with the object of appealing to Mr George Smith, who was actually in the building at the time he arrived, but Mr Smith would not see him . . .

As a postscript to Ivy Holgate's account it may be mentioned here that besides his annotated copy of the *Life* there are two further links with Sidney Biddell in the Parsonage. In 1883 Ellen Nussey gave him a tiny black edged envelope containing a lock of Charlotte's hair. At an auction after Biddell's death this relic was bought by the American collector, Henry Bonnell, who presented it to the Brontë Society in 1916.

There is also a pencil drawing by Charlotte of Miss Wooler's school at Roe Head. The drawing was given by Mr Brontë to Martha Brown as a keepsake which later passed to one of her sisters who sold it to Biddell in 1881. At the same auction after Biddell's death Mr Bonnell was again the buyer and the drawing returned to the parsonage as part of the Bonnell Collection bequest in 1928.

21

Reminiscences of Emma Huidekoper Cortazzo, 1866–1882

Brontë Society *Transactions* 13.Pt 3.220 (1958)

In 1938 Mrs Helen Greene Arnold, of Boston, Massachusetts, who at that time was the Brontë Society's Honorary American Representative, discovered through a neighbour that a few miles from her summer home there lived in Newport an elderly fellow member of the Society, Katherine Renée Cortazzo. A meeting of the two ladies was quickly arranged at which Katherine Cortazzo recalled that at the age of fifteen in 1882 she went with her mother, Emma Cullum Huidekoper Cortazzo, to visit Ellen Nussey, who was then living at Fieldhead, Birstall.

Further visits followed, and sometimes mother and daughter stayed overnight listening to Ellen's accounts of the Brontë family and handling bundles of Charlotte's letters.

Emma Huidekoper had as a child of ten been captivated by *Jane Eyre* and years later when, after an illness, she was sent to Italy to regain her health, she had already determined to make a Brontë pilgrimage. While in Rome she became engaged to an Italian artist named Cortazzo, who acted as escort when she and her chaperone left for England in June 1866, and within a few days she arrived at the Black Bull. Her notes and journal recording this visit and a subsequent visit in 1882 were in due course made available to Mrs Greene Arnold who compiled the following account.

'Behold me, then,' wrote Emma, 'after years of longing and waiting at last in the West Riding of Yorkshire.' Could they have rooms at the Black Bull Inn and something to eat? She (Mrs Sugden) took time to consider ... she had, she informed us, in broad Yorkshire dialect, 'ad aboon a 'undred to a funeral and a tea fight the nicht an' the 'ouse were all of a muck an' a muddle.' The room and food were provided, however, and Emma describes 'the small but tidy bedroom, the immense mahogany four-poster piled high with feather beds and hung about with green moreen curtains . . . the portable steps, the old-fashioned high-backed chairs polished to a mirror-like brightness, and on the walls a series of grim portraits, central among them a stately lady in blue satin and Flanders lace who stared stonily into the recesses of the four-poster, suggesting the possibilities of ghostly visitation. On this, her first visit to Haworth, Emma saw the church and the parsonage essentially as it was in the Brontës' time. 'Save for the replacing with modern and larger glass of the small, old-fashioned panes in the windows, the house externally at least had undergone no change.' To her keen disappointment, their request to see the interior of the house, or at least the lower rooms, was emphatically refused, not once but twice.

Pleading with the servant on their second attempt the following morning . . . 'a harsh voice from within was heard bidding her 'shut the door'; no one, she explained, was ever allowed to see the rooms. Even a request to make a tiny sketch from the garden was rudely refused and we were forced to turn away, in deep disappointment.'

Sixteen years were to pass before Emma, now Madame Cortazzo, again made her way to the Brontë country, taking with her on this visit her only child, the fifteen-year-old Katharine Renée. Her stay in Haworth at this time is of peculiar interest because she then met many persons who had known the Brontë family. Moreover, ' . . . I was to make an acquaintance which rapidly ripened into warmest friendship with that 'friend of friends', the beloved 'E' of the letters, Charlotte's constant correspondent till her death, Miss Ellen Nussey.

> 'The day was grey and showery, though it was July, when I reached Haworth. This time there was no long drive from Keighley, with the grey village always in sight, preparing one for the bleakness of its situation and the ruggedness of its aspect. A small branch line from Keighley brings the moorland village into easier access, and the pale of modernity. Yet it still seems to shrink from being dragged into too close relations with its huge neighbours, Bradford and Keighley, and still to desire to hold itself aloof from the larger outer world. The little station stands in the middle of a field, and there was no sign of life about it when we left the train, which moved quietly away through the rain and mist as though trying to make as little noise and disturbance as possible. We found no conveyance ready, and a solitary porter seemed rather to shrink from than court our notice.
>
> 'However, a shock-headed youth appeared who took our bags and we started. The climb was toilsome at best in the drizzling rain and stormy

gusts of wind from the moors that beat us about. A final and sudden turn brought us into the High Street, and a little further into the square before the Black Bull inn which I found as weather beaten, as grey and forbidding as of yore. The boy put the bags on the floor and while I sought a sixpence from a pocket under my dripping mackintosh, he disappeared without a word and was seen no more.

'Mrs Sugden said with Yorkshire brevity when I inquired if she had a room, 'Yes, surely,' and when we reached it she merely asked, 'Do ye stay the nicht?' and so disappeared. We quickly divested ourselves of wet wraps and sat down to take breath after our uphill walk. For a time there was diversion enough in just looking from the window which gave on the square. Indifferent to the rain, the people clattered by in their wooden shoes. Two toddlers, bare necked and bare armed, stood hand-in-hand looking wistfully into the window of a bake shop, where a tempting array of loaves round and square, of tea cakes and currant buns and seed and plum cakes, rivetted their gaze. The Vicar passed by with his curate in earnest conversation... a huge cart-horse struggled upward with a heavy load, slipping backward at almost every step of the steep way, while the carter in dingy smock walked at his head and sought to ease and encourage his beast. Grimy mill hands passed, taciturn and grave; a man with a squealing pig had difficulties in driving the porker who bolted into every lane and doorway; our landlady could be seen at the tap-room window... the draper next door came to his window to watch the pig's divagations...'

Later Mme. Cortazzo and her daughter ventured forth in the rain, '... to ramble and to note the changes in church and vicarage of which we had heard, but no preparation for which could save us the pang of disappointment and regret we felt, as we looked at the altered aspect of both.'

In the light of later developments and present restorations* it is of special interest to note her prophetic words:

'There may have been need to build a more commodious church; why not then have also built a new rectory and left the old, unhealthy house weather-worn and aged, to its memories and associations with the years of weary waiting and disappointment and struggle, with the brief span of brilliant success and fame, with the short intervals of health, but with longer periods of trial, sickness and suffering that marked the lives of the Brontës. The present state of things is regrettable; one can but

* A reference by Helen Greene Arnold to the alterations at the Parsonage completed in 1959.

hope that one day this rectory, so dear to many, may take on a final character of a Museum to house the precious relics that posterity will surely gather somewhere to perpetuate the cult of geniuses of quite peculiar order.

'It was too late to ramble further, so we returned to high tea at the Inn... the keen moorland air had whetted our appetites so that we did full justice to the viands provided – a round of cold beef, crisp rashers of bacon, hot tea cakes with plenty of jam and marmalade. I sat again later in the queer three-cornered chair sipping my tea, listening vaguely to the chatter of the landlady's parrot, and the clatter of clogs in the flagged passage, while I mused on the changes that time brings and planned my further visitings... the long twilight permitted another stroll, so I went out to seek two persons who had been occasional assistants in the Brontë household, Mrs Tabitha Ratcliffe and Mrs Sarah Wood, sister and cousin respectively of that Martha Brown who for so many years rendered faithful service at Haworth Rectory.

'I was directed to Stubbin Lane* and to reach it went down the steep High Street... I found Mrs Ratcliffe in a tiny cottage in the Hebden Bridge Road and was warmly welcomed by her, after I stated the object of my visit, this being to see certain relics of the Brontës which I had been told were in her possession. She seated me in an ancient rocking chair in her kitchen or living room, while she went upstairs to get her 'bits of things'. During her absence I had leisure to admire the homely comfort of this ordinary country kitchen – the bright fire on the shining grate, the glistening brass kettle singing its cheerful song, the tall clock in its polished case, the work-table under the lattice window, and the several chairs of ancient form, notably the rocking chair very common in Yorkshire.

'Mrs Ratcliffe settled to the showing of her 'bits of things' with loving fervour, spreading them on the table to my view. A little wooden foot stool** and an inkstained writing desk seemed, she said, to go together, for 'Miss Emily always carried the stool into the garden or put it before the kitchen fire and then put the desk on her knee when she was about writing.' An old rosewood workbox was the next exhibit, lined with blue satin and showing its many compartments where bobbins and winders might be kept by the careful Anne, to whom it belonged. It held now a tiny square of Berlin wool work, a dainty bit of cambric, a few

* Now Sun Street.

** Most of the objects mentioned here and in the following paragraphs are now in the Brontë Parsonage Museum.

pearly shells gathered, perhaps, on the sands of Scarborough during her last days, all trifles but singularly suggestive of the rare delicacy and daintiness of their former owner. There was next a little porcelain smelling-bottle, a vinaigrette bearing the initials M.B. in gilt on the back, formerly belonging to the mother of the Brontës. This had been loved and used by Anne. After Anne's death Charlotte had given it to Martha Brown as being especially associated with her sister. A daguerreotype* came to light now, which I eagerly seized upon. Mrs Ratcliffe said that the likenesses were not perfect. Still, one got an impression of what the sisters were like when it was made. Charlotte's face is familiar to us through the reproductions of the portrait by Richmond, but of the appearance of the other sisters we have less accurate knowledge and must largely rely on our mental picture, on the descriptions of Mrs Gaskell and others. In this faded picture Anne presents a regular profile, beautiful wavy hair in curls about her neck, finely arched eyebrows and a delicate, sensitive mouth. Charlotte's face seemed to me quite unlike the portrait affixed to the *Life*, showing her at an earlier age, but I think it could never have been a good likeness, since it gives her face a square contour which it never had. Emily's features were not easily made out, as a crack in the glass crossed them, but one detects the same arched eyebrows as Anne, with fine eyes and hair parted on the side and falling in a graceful way over her forehead, this recalling exactly the description of Shirley Keeldar, of whom we are told Emily was in some sort the original.

The three sisters are similarly dressed in plain frocks, cut half low in the neck, with muslin kerchiefs crossed on the breast and with the gigot sleeves of their time. There was also a recent likeness of Mr Nicholls, showing a portly man, not in clerical dress, bearded and broad-faced, a country gentleman, which he has become.

From Mrs Ratcliffe's I sought out Mrs Sarah Wood, another who in former years lent aid on occasions at the Rectory. The slightly cold and repellent air, so often noticeable in Yorkshire folk, and the reserve with which in this instance I was received, soon gave way when she found I was a genuine lover of the Brontës. Her plain face lighted, her manner warmed, as she showed me the very few but interesting relics she possessed and told me readily of those olden days and lovingly recalled

* This is probably the photograph on glass of Branwell's 'Pillar Portrait' taken by a Haworth photographer mentioned by Mrs Ellis Chadwick in her *In the Footsteps of the Brontës* (London: Sir Isaac Pitman & Sons Ltd, 1914). See also *The art of the Brontës* by Christine Alexander and Jane Sellars (p. 312).

one detail after another of the quiet life at Haworth Rectory. She touched with reverent fingers the little worn black slippers that had been Charlotte's and the white under-bodice that was in her wedding outfit, and also a very fine cambric handkerchief spotted with pink and marked A.B. in the corner in cross-stitch, with the date. Lastly there was an old japanned coffee-pot, which she turned about to show me, scratched on the bottom 'E.Brontë, Haworth Parsonage' while its sides bore initials, dates, rough profiles and odd sketches.

'She were always scribblin' and writin', were Miss Emily,' said Mrs Wood, 'Many is the time I've seen her in t'kitchen, waitin' for t' kettle t'boil, or t'bread to bake, scribblin' away on bits o'paper.'

'Charlotte's name appeared also on the coffee-pot in her own delicate handwriting and there was an A.B., evidently Anne's writing, among the numerous evidences of Emily's restless habit of 'scribblin'.

On another day Mme Cortazzo 'went to see at Saltaire, Bradford, a number of articles which had belonged to the Brontës and which had been given by Mr Nicholls to Martha Brown, who had died a year or more ago. She had left these relics to her brother-in-law who kindly showed them to me. There were many early drawings of the sisters', drawings of feet and ears and arms and hands, such as from drawing-books young people used to be given as models to copy. Then came more elaborate efforts – a copy of Hogarth's *Idle Apprentices* by Branwell, a small landscape copied with wonderful fidelity, from some small engravings, by Charlotte. Unless closely examined, it seemed impossible it was not an engraving. A spirited water-colour was by Emily of Flossy,* Anne's dog, a brown and white spaniel, chasing a bird over the moor. There were many small drawings of Charlotte's, executed with extreme minuteness and delicacy; several letters were shown, too, of C.B. and a lock of old Mr Brontë's hair, white as snow and fine as spun silk. Charlotte's hair was pale brown.'

At Bradford Mme Cortazzo called upon old Nancy Wainwright, then over seventy, who lived with Mr and Mrs Brontë at Thornton and went with them to Haworth. One had no need to question her, for she talked on with the garrulity of age. 'Mrs Brontë wa'n't pretty, but she was gentle as ever were, and a kind mistress... she suffered, did Mrs Brontë, for ye know she died of a cancer an' it were a long time workin' on her. Miss Branwell were another soart, she were so crosslike

* The dog was given to Anne when a governess at Thorp Green. It survived its mistress by more than five years.

an' fault findin' and so close, she ga'e us, my sister Sarah an' me, but a gill o' beer a day, an' she gi'e to us hersel', did Miss Branwell, to our dinner, she wouldn'a let us go to draw it oursel' in t'cellar. A pint a day she gi'e us, that were half a pint for me an' half a pint for Sarah... Charlotte were a sharp child. Why, one day when she were a sma' bairn at Thornton, her faither went away to preach an' the vicar from Bradford comed to tak' his place and he were a stiff-made gentleman, he were, an' Charlotte said right to his face, 'I don't like this gentleman, Mamma, he swaggers so.' Then I had to tak' her from t'room, for there were no knowin' what she'd say next. Mr Brontë were aye a kind man.'

In that same year Mme Cortazzo turned her steps from Haworth to other scenes. 'I knew several families in Bradford,' she writes, 'and was most hospitably received and everything was done to further the object of my coming to Yorkshire. Among fellow guests one had known Mr Grant, Vicar of Oxenhope, the original of the curate Donne... another guest offered me a card of introduction to Mr T. Wemyss Reid, which I most gladly accepted, and it was to the kindness of this gentleman that I owed the presentation to Miss Ellen Nussey, that devoted friend of the Brontës who cherishes their memory so devotedly and whom I am privileged to call a most valued friend of my own, since many years, following upon my first going to see her at Fieldhead, Birstall. To this modest house high on the hillside above the village she had removed from Laneside, Gomersal, some two years before, and thither I bent my steps one day in high anticipation...

'Miss Nussey was out, but the maid asked us to wait, which we did. It is a tiny house, very simple, very neat and full of sunlight. The little parlour with its cheerful outlook over the valley towards Birstall, its neutral tint of paper and furniture, the quaint portraits on the walls and the pretty water-colours here and there, quite charmed me. We sat a long time waiting for Miss Nussey to return, and when she came I was in such an agitated state that for a few minutes I could scarcely talk intelligently. She is a lovely, gentle lady with soft grey eyes, hair wavy and nearly white though still quite thick, delicate complexion, sweet cheeks that one longed to kiss. She was dressed in a sober-hued brown silk dress, very well worn and rather out of date, but suiting her to perfection. She received us most cordially and almost at once began to speak of Miss Brontë. At first, as was right, she spoke with what I can scarcely call reserve, but perhaps timidly, tho' that does not quite express it either; at any rate, as soon as she found me an earnestly eager and attentive listener, she spoke with great freedom and told me so much of Miss B and her sisters that I was filled with delight.

'The long summer day passed all too quickly for an insatiable listener who eagerly absorbed the pictures of the past that were painted in words by one who was a part of that life at Haworth 40 years ago. The grey Rectory, the old parson, Charlotte, Emily and Anne, the curates, the sexton – all were painted for me in vivid colours. Also memories moved to Birstall, to Moor Lane, where amid a wider and more cheerful circle, some of Miss Brontë's happiest days were passed; where at 'curling hair time' over the bedroom fire, she held communion with her 'dearest Nell.' It was for me a very solemn thing to hear a participator of these communings recount them to my humble self, and I have ever treasured all I was told of this and much else'...

Fortunately for those of us who share Emma Cortazzo's Brontë interest, she recorded at once in detail all that Miss Nussey told her. From these notes we realise how much of the information regarding the Brontë family Mrs Gaskell had obtained first-hand from Ellen Nussey. Much of this is now familiar, but there is a freshness, a feeling of intimacy in the closely packed pages of her journal that lends vividness to her descriptions:

'I hardly know how to group together the pictures of the past which have been presented in my mind's eye through repeated visits and talks at the fireside of Miss Ellen Nussey. What we owe to this gentle lady, living retired on her Yorkshire moor, one can easily realise, for if we take from Mrs Gaskell's *Life* and from Mr T.W.Reid's monograph the letters written by Charlotte to her friend 'E' and the data given by her – what would remain? A few bare facts and dates. All that renders these books so vividly interesting; all that lends such intense charm to that strange life would be wanting. The Brontës knew few people, *so* few intimately that the term can scarcely be applied to anyone but Miss Nussey. Others might know Charlotte as authoress or as the parson's daughter, but no one ever knew her to her heart's core as did 'E' and no one ever came so close to those shy sisters, Emily and Anne, as this gentle friend. To her, even Emily unbent and showed somewhat of what she carried beneath the icy exterior she showed to the world... The timid shrinking Anne loved the gentle 'E'. She loved her in life, wished to have her with her as death drew near, and looked to her to sustain, care for and encourage Charlotte when she should be no more'...

'Looking back nearly one hundred years to that first visit of young Emma to Haworth,' Helen Arnold concluded, 'we realise that she was a pioneer, certainly the first American in the field of Brontë research. Deeply and sincerely devoted to this subject as she was, we can understand the joyous enthusiasm of a young girl who of her last moments at Haworth, on this first pilgrimage, records:–

> 'In a fold on the moor among heather and broom, near an old stone quarry. Here, away from the wind, we could draw breath and lie upon the stubbly down just as the sisters used to do. I could well understand, after that, the passion for the moors that they all felt, and how one of them sickened and pined when long absent from them. I fretted against going down again to the haunts of men, away from that great freedom and the wind rushing past in its ceaseless blowing.'

22

Haworth, November 1904 by Virginia Woolf

Brontë Society *Transactions* 17.Pt 4.272 (1979)

Virginia Woolf was hardly an early visitor to Haworth. By 1904 the Brontë Society was in its eleventh year, but it seems appropriate that these varying impressions of the home of the Brontës should conclude with those of a young woman of 22 whose own literary career was about to unfold. At the time of her visit she was staying at Giggleswick with a cousin who was Headmaster of the school.

Her account became her first published piece of writing; it appeared on 21 December 1904 in a London weekly newspaper *The Guardian*, which catered for a clerical public. In 1916 she wrote a piece on *Jane Eyre* and *Wuthering Heights* which was subsequently reprinted in *The Common Reader*, a miscellaneous collection of her papers published in 1925.

By 1904 there was a new Rector at Haworth and she was permitted to enter the parsonage. It is clear that she was not at the time entirely in favour of literary museums:

> I do not know whether pilgrimages to the shrines of famous men ought not to be condemned as sentimental journeys. It is better to read Carlyle in your own study chair than to visit the sound-proof room and pore over the manuscripts at Chelsea. I should be inclined to set an examination on Frederick the Great in place of entrance fee; only, in that case the house would soon have to be shut up. The curiosity is only legitimate when the house of a great writer or the country in which it is set adds something to our understanding of his books. This justification you have for a pilgrimage to the home and country of Charlotte Brontë and her sisters.
>
> The *Life*, by Mrs Gaskell, gives you the impression that Haworth and the Brontës are somehow inextricably mixed. Haworth expresses the

Brontës; the Brontës express Haworth; they fit like a snail to its shell. How far surroundings radically affect people's minds, it is not for me to ask; superficially, the influence is great, but it is worth asking if the famous parsonage had been placed in a London slum, the dens of Whitechapel would not have had the same result as the lonely Yorkshire moors. However, I am taking away my only excuse for visiting Haworth. Unreasonable or not, one of the chief points of a recent visit to Yorkshire was that an expedition to Haworth could be accomplished. The necessary arrangements were made, and we determined to take advantage of the first day for our expedition. A real northern snowstorm had been doing the honours of the moors. It was rash to wait for fine weather, and it was also cowardly. I understand that the sun very seldom shone on the Brontë family, and if we chose a really fine day we should have to make allowance for the fact that fifty years ago there were few fine days at Haworth, and that we were, therefore, for the sake of comfort, rubbing out half the shadows in the picture. However, it would be interesting to see what impression Haworth could make upon the brilliant weather of Settle. We certainly passed through a very cheerful land, which might be likened to a vast wedding cake, of which the icing was slightly undulating; the earth was bridal in its virgin snow, which helped to suggest the comparison.

Keighley is often mentioned in the *Life*; it was the big town four miles from Haworth in which Charlotte used to make her more important purchases – her wedding gown, perhaps, and the thin little cloth boots which we examined under glass in the Brontë Museum. It is a big manufacturing town, hard and stony, and clattering with business, in the way of these Northern towns. They make small provision for the sentimental traveller, and our only occupation was to picture the slight figure of Charlotte trotting along the streets in her thin mantle, hustled into the gutter by more burly passers-by. It was the Keighley of her day, and that was some comfort. Our excitement as we neared Haworth had in it an element of suspense that was really painful, as though we were to meet some long-separated friend, who might have changed in the interval – so clear an image of Haworth had we from print and picture. At a certain point we entered the valley, up both sides of which the village climbs, and right on the hill-top, looking down over its parish, we saw the famous oblong tower of the church. This marked the shrine at which we were to do homage.

It may have been the effect of a sympathetic imagination, but I think that there were good reasons why Haworth did certainly strike one not exactly as gloomy, but, what is worse for artistic purposes, as dingy and commonplace. The houses, built of yellow-brown stone, date from the early nineteenth century. They climb the moor step by step in little detached strips, some distance apart, so that the town instead of making one compact blot on the landscape has contrived to get a whole stretch into its clutches. There is a long line of houses up the moor-side, which clusters round the church and parsonage with a little clump of trees. At the top the interest for a Brontë lover becomes suddenly intense. The church, the parsonage, the Brontë Museum, the school where Charlotte taught, and the Bull Inn [*sic*] where Branwell drank, are all within a stone's throw of each other. The museum is certainly rather a pallid and inanimate collection of objects. An effort ought to be made to keep things out of these mausoleums, but the choice often lies between them and destruction, so that we must be grateful for the care which has preserved much that is, under any circumstances, of deep interest. Here are many autograph letters, pencil drawings, and other documents. But the most touching case – so touching that one hardly feels reverent in one's gaze – is that which contains the little personal relics, the dresses and shoes of the dead woman. The natural fate of such things is to die before the body that wore them, and because these, trifling and transient though they are, have survived, Charlotte Brontë the woman comes to life, and one forgets the chiefly memorable fact that she was a great writer. Her shoes and her thin muslin dress have outlived her. One other object gives a thrill; the little oak stool which Emily carried with her on her solitary moorland tramps, and on which she sat, if not to write, as they say, to think what was probably better than her writing.

The church, of course, save part of the tower, is renewed since Brontë days; but that remarkable churchyard remains. The old edition of the *Life* had on its title page a little print which struck the keynote of the book; it seemed to be all graves – gravestones stood ranked all round; you walked on a pavement lettered with dead names; the graves had solemnly invaded the garden of the parsonage itself, which was a little oasis of life in the midst of the dead. This is no exaggeration of the artist's, as we found; the stones seem to start out of the ground at you in tall upright lines, like an army of silent soldiers. There is no hand's breadth untenanted; indeed, the economy of space is somewhat irreverent. In old days a flagged path, which suggested the slabs of graves, led from the front door of the parsonage to the churchyard without interruption of wall or hedge; the garden was practically the graveyard too; the successors of the Brontës, however, wishing a little space between life and death, planted a hedge and several tall trees, which now cut off the parsonage garden completely. The house is precisely the same as it was in Charlotte's day, save that one new wing has been added. It is easy to shut the eye to this, and then you have the square, boxlike parsonage, built of the ugly, yellow-brown stone which they quarry from the moors behind, precisely as it was when Charlotte lived and died there. Inside, of course, the changes are many, though not such as to obscure the original shape of the rooms. There is nothing remarkable in a mid-Victorian parsonage, though tenanted by genius, and the only room which awakens curiosity is the kitchen, now used as an ante-room, in which the girls tramped as they conceived their work One other spot has a certain grim interest – the oblong recess beside the staircase into which Emily drove her bulldog during the famous fight, and pinned him while she pummelled him. It is otherwise a little sparse parsonage, much like others of its kind. It was due to the courtesy of the present incumbent that we were allowed to inspect it; in his place I should often feel inclined to exorcise the three famous ghosts.

One thing only remained; the church in which Charlotte worshipped, was married and lies buried. Here, though much is altered, a few things remain to tell of her. The slab which bears the names of the succession of children and of their parents – their births and deaths – strikes the eye first. Name follows name, Maria the mother, Maria the daughter, Elizabeth, Branwell, Emily, Anne, Charlotte, and lastly the old father, who outlived them all. Emily was only thirty years old, and Charlotte but nine years older. 'The sting of death is sin, and the strength of sin is the law, but thanks be to God which giveth us the victory through our Lord Jesus Christ.' That is the inscription which has been placed beneath their names, and with reason; for however harsh the struggle, Emily, and Charlotte above all, fought to victory.